The Art *of* Golf Design

To purchase prints of artwork contained in this book visit
www.scottsdalecollection.com or call (301) 765-0074.

www.sleepingbearpress.com

Printed and bound in Canada.

10 9 8 7 6 5 4 3 2 1

Library of Congress Cataloging-in-Publication Data

Miller, Michael G.
The art of golf design / golf landscapes by Michael G. Miller ;
essays by Geoff Shackelford.
p. cm.
ISBN 1-886947-30-9
Golf courses—Design and construction.
2. Golf course architects. I. Shackelford, Geoff. II. Title.
GV975 .M55 2001
712'.5—dc21
2001040073

∾

The Art *of* Golf Design

GOLF LANDSCAPES *by* MICHAEL G. MILLER

ESSAYS *by* GEOFF SHACKELFORD

Sleeping Bear Press

WHY GOLF IS ART AND ART IS GOLF

WE HAVE NOT FAR TO SEEK—

SO MUCH DEPENDS UPON THE LIE,

SO MUCH UPON THE CLEEK.

∾

RUDYARD KIPLING

Foreword

BY MICHAEL G. MILLER

The concept of painting historical landscapes of golf holes designed by the world's greatest architects evolved quite naturally from a single event.

Author Geoff Shackelford had asked that I paint a cover for his then upcoming book on George C. Thomas Jr., *The Captain*. We chose the sixth hole at Riviera, circa 1927. This painting viewed well and the idea for this book sprang to life.

The paintings reproduced herein are based largely on black and white photographs of the period depicted. This method allowed me great latitude in portraying the time of day, the season, and the weather. This, however, was not the case regarding the design features of each hole. The architecture demanded factual accuracy, sometimes gained with much difficulty, in the rendering of green complexes, approaches, fairway contours, bunkers, and water. These features were not idealized, exaggerated, or romanticized.

This endeavor has been not only personally fulfilling, but a perfect vehicle for learning and gaining knowledge of the great thinkers of golf architecture and their unparalleled creations.

It is my hope the reader will come to appreciate, as I have been fortunate enough to do, that the application of the principles that govern fine art, in fact, govern fine golf design. This understanding, as delineated in the essays to follow, gives rise to a great pleasure in viewing and playing exceptional golf designs. It is a pleasure that can last a lifetime.

Artwork

Essays and Sidebars

Golf architecture is not a science. Creatively it is not amenable to measurable knowledge. The failure to understand this is one reason responsible for the dilemma in the minds of most golfers who try to come to a logical understanding of golf architecture and get nowhere.

MAX BEHR

What Is Art In Golf Architecture?

What is art in golf architecture?

It is easy to fall back on the modern day tendency of declaring "to each his own," and leaving matters peaceful to avoid heated discussions or insulting a friend's home course.

Yes, we all have our own preferences and each of us finds beauty in different types of art. But as with other pursuits, time has a clever way of separating the genuine architectural masterworks from simpler, less interesting design efforts. After each new course we visit it becomes apparent that certain courses are singular. It becomes evident that some designs evoke certain emotions and provide dramatic situations, while others may function well but ultimately fail to elicit much interest.

In the last 100 years three general principles of golf architecture have emerged as the linchpins for any artistic effort. The art of building a course certainly cannot be confined to perfecting these three traits and leaving matters at that. Many factors influence the golf architect's canvas. But time has shown that these three elements are the key components of the most revered designs.

We are referring to the manner in which *naturalness*, *variety*, and *strategy* are melded together by the architect and presented for the golfer to encounter.

Every architect or developer trying to create a special course defines how these three elements are carried out differently. Yet, the real answer to understanding each trait can be found in a close study of certain courses, even if different designers with distinct styles created those great designs.

The intent of this book is to bring forth a modern day perspective on what constitutes genuine art in golf architecture and how to return the best elements to golf architecture. We hope to reinforce a few timeless truths and decipher the classic layouts from those masquerading as art. We also want to open your willing eyes to golf architecture's possibilities. Most of all, this book hopes to fuel your passion for the unique landscapes of golf.

We also know that these are lofty goals, because as mentioned previously, each golfer has their own take on this interactive art form. Our senses react differently to a variety of design styles and some of us just don't react at all, merely taking pleasure in good conditioning, a friendly golf course staff, or the company of friends. In no way do we discourage that view of golf. We are merely attempting to convey the time-tested principles found in certain courses that are widely held as masterpieces.

Golf architecture is an art form like no other because layouts are constantly evolving and they (can) play dramatically different each day. Change in other art forms is far more gradual, and significant alterations to the artist's vision are not tolerated. In golf architecture, the designer's work is frequently altered, rarely for the correct reasons and usually with poor outcomes.

When creating a golf course, the architect and his team must incorporate function, design strategy, aesthetic preferences, engineering expertise, agronomics, and complex governmental regulations. Yet at the same time the architect must create something that is attractive to look at, playable for as many golfers as possible, and still try to make it original in spirit by incorporating natural features. It is not an easy task, particularly in a pursuit where the clients usually demand much more artistic input than in other quests.

Once the course is built, the superintendent and local golfers must find the always-sensitive balance between maintaining excellent playing conditions while presenting the course in a way that reflects the architect's artistic style and strategic philosophy. It is never an easy task making art and science meet. Therefore, the examples of inspiring golf architecture and creative maintenance combining to flourish for a long period of time are all too rare. Many elements must be dealt with handily to create a course of individual integrity. But as demonstrated in Mike Miller's landscape paintings throughout this book, there are fine examples where, as George Thomas wrote, "art and utility meet."

Again, this is not to discount the notion that each of us is entitled to our own artistic taste or that courses have to be museum pieces to be properly enjoyed. We simply believe that with the resources poured into modern golf construction and the exciting possibilities laid out by our ancestors, that quality golf architecture should be more widespread. And we also believe that the future should be open to new and exciting design possibilities that will exceed our wildest dreams, as long as the golfing public has even the most basic understanding of architecture.

Master architects like Alister MacKenzie, A. W. Tillinghast, and George Thomas believed that the art of golf design would develop in unimaginable ways. Actually it has, but just not in the dramatic, artistic, or inspirational manner that they predicted. In fact, golf saw several decades where architects mysteriously distanced themselves from the masters and created supposedly "original" approaches, which have since proved to have limited appeal when the novelty wore off or the course's assembly-line style of construction became apparent.

As Faulkner pointed out, "the past is never dead, it's not even past." And in a sport filled with more tradition and history than just about any other, there is a disturbing modern day propensity to claim that one is creating courses in the spirit of the old architects. Yet a look at the architecture claiming to be inspired by masterworks usually reveals a complete refusal to appreciate the charisma and genius of the masters. Worse, the claims are made even while the architect proves incapable of reproducing basic principles such as irregularity, variety, strategy, or naturalness.

It is our desire to revisit those common principles through essays, architect sketches, and most of all, Mike Miller's landscape paintings. Yes, we have our own preferences for certain artistic efforts, but our tastes are based on a historical perspective that takes into account where the game has been and how it has evolved. And we believe the principles that lead to lasting art in golf architecture have virtually disappeared from the modern game known as golf.

The goal of combining Miller's paintings with essays on design is to augment your golfing insight and make the courses you play that much more interesting to study and discuss. We hope the images and essays here put a new twist on the subject of golf architecture and aid your efforts to spot timeless traits and design elements you did not previously notice.

We are convinced that "beautiful" courses feel and look as if they were found. That the grass was merely cut down amidst the wild, rustic hazards for the purpose of playing the game, even if it took hard work and many months (or years) of construction to create such a look.

We have no doubt that the most enduring holes ask you to think and tempt you to try risky shots. They ask you to make tough decisions and the great holes excite your senses with their unusual, sometimes even quirky charm.

And we are certain that maintenance and the setup of courses must not try to control the game, but instead that luck is a charming part of golf and must not be eliminated in the name of fairness. Trying to abolish luck from the game is nearly always at the expense of creating dramatic golf holes.

Mostly, we hope to provoke constructively critical discussion on the variety of design styles because no art form can truly be savored if there isn't plenty of healthy discussion about its strengths and weaknesses.

The essays here attempt to reflect the principles of the master architects from the 1920s while also taking into account the evolution and future of golf. Certain courses such as Pine Valley, Cypress Point, and Merion do tend to appear more consistently, but also featured prominently is Sand Hills, the modern masterpiece by Bill Coore and Ben Crenshaw.

We have included brief contributions from many of our favorite architects who preached the necessity to study and build courses with an artistic approach. In particular, the words of Alister MacKenzie, Robert Hunter, Max Behr, George Thomas, Tom Simpson, and even some anonymous characters from the early part of the century are featured.

Thankfully, there is genuine artistry to be found in some modern layouts. There is an expanding audience of golfers who seek out and appreciate the special touches injected by architects, and this audience explains why there is some semblance of a renaissance movement today. Better yet, with just a little more study, chances are that a full-fledged design renaissance could occur: a twenty-first century revival that witnesses a return to artistic designs which golfers can enjoy at a fair price.

Of late, it has become popular for some supposedly learned people in the game to equate the spotting of "great" golf course design to the late Justice Potter Stewart's line about pornography—you know, not being able to define it but "knowing it when you see it." However, we think that is a shallow way out for people of intelligence who simply don't want to take the time to study golf architecture and support their opinions. Sure, we all love certain things for reasons we may not know and no one can argue against the powerful influence of sheer beauty in golf design. But that should be the mere beginning of our exploration into golf architecture, particularly for these "experts." We should know something worth studying when we see it, and then begin the analysis and discussion of that architecture for the betterment of the art.

The self-important "I know it when I see it" approach to judging golf courses is one of the reasons that golf architecture has forfeited many of the high standards established by the MacKenzies and Tillinghasts of the world. Despite advances in construction, education, and maintenance, the reliance on "experts" knowing it "when they see it" is the main reason this art has failed to attain the widespread excellence that many of the master architects predicted would occur. It is the primary reason that politics and the exclusivity of a club are given so much weight when looking at the various modern day rankings, and why the architecture is coming a distant second to "experience" related elements.

However, we also strongly believe that a majority of golfers have not been given a fair chance to learn about the best of golf course design, either in the form of "museum-caliber" courses available to all golfers, or in the form of educational books, essays, and illustrations. Oddly, golf architecture is a subject that requires just a little time and effort to understand the basics. And even when the golfer has only a fundamental understanding of the art, its yields are everlasting.

What Is Art in Golf Architecture?

BY MAX BEHR, 1927

We are too apt to mistake that which is pretty, or picturesque, for the beautiful. Prettiness, although pleasing, is a transient thing incident to the fancies of the moment; but beauty rests upon the fundamental—its lineaments are the surface revelation of a perfection that lies beneath. Where beauty is lacking there must likewise be a lack of intelligence. Indeed, beauty may well prove to be the economic solvent to that continual evolution in the way of innovations and alterations to which most all golf courses are subject. If the holes have been most advantageously routed in the beginning, beauty should then be the ideal to be striven for in construction, for beauty practically always accompanies economy of structure. When we perceive it, we first become aware of truth; and only in the presence of truth do we recognize stability and permanence.

What, then, is art in golf architecture? What are the values we should seek, and the method we should adopt to arrive at them?

If we examine courses in general, we shall find that wherever the modifications of the ground have been so inwrought as to seem inevitably a part of their surroundings, not only are they liable to manifest beauty, but we can be relatively sure the work promises to endure. Experience has taught us that courses constructed with no higher end than merely to create a playground around which one may strike a ball, present the golfer with little more than a landscape brutalized with the ideas of some other golfer.

We forget that the playing of golf should be a delightful expression of freedom. Indeed, the perfect rhythmic coordination of the muscles to swing the club makes of the golf stroke an art. And, being such, it is apt to induce an emotional state, under the stress of which human nature is not rational, and resents outspoken criticism. It follows that when the canvas of Nature over which the club-stroke must pass is filled with holes artificially designed to impede the golfer's progress, these obvious man-made contraptions cause a violation of that sense of liberty he has every right to expect. This accounts for the checkered history of every artificial appearing golf course.

But, if we look closely, we shall discover that the changes rarely involve natural hazards. Indeed, the veriest tyro is unconsciously aware that golf is a contest with Nature. Thus, where he meets her unadorned, unblemished by the hand of man, he meets her without criticism.

Golf architecture is not an art of representation; it is, essentially, an art of interpretation. And an interpretative art allows freedom to fancy only through obedience to the law which dominates its medium, a law that lies outside ourselves. The medium of the artist is paint, and he becomes its master; but the medium of the golf architect is the surface of the earth over which the forces of Nature alone are master.

Therefore, in the prosecution of his designs, if the architect correctly uses the forces of nature to express them and thus succeeds in hiding his hand, then, only, has he created the illusion that can still all criticism.

LATE AFTERNOON, THIRTEENTH AT CYPRESS POINT, CIRCA 1929: *Cypress Point took three years of organizational planning and only five months to build. Most would assume this masterpiece might have taken an opposite route to completion with years of construction to create the wondrous landscape we know to be Cypress Point. However, once construction started in the fall of 1927, Cypress Point came about rather quickly. Robert Hunter was the on-site construction supervisor and associate architect to Alister MacKenzie. The thirteenth hole, as depicted here, may have been their finest moment artistically. Note how the 380-yard par-4 hole blends almost imperceptibly into the dunescape. The dramatic greenside bunkers feel overwhelming when standing on the green, yet they were not created until very near the course's unofficial opening in August of 1928. Historic photographs show that MacKenzie and Hunter had not touched the berm-like ridge surrounding the green. Instead, they were going to leave it as a natural dune, a state the area appears in even when the course is grown-in during the summer of 1928. However, in the initial photos showing the course open for play, the architects and shapers had since defined the dunes into bunkers, perhaps to stabilize the area and also likely for dramatic effect. Their "last minute" decision was a wise one. Is there a more stunning example of a golf hole blending imperceptibly into its terrain than Cypress Point's thirteenth?*

Late Afternoon, Thirteenth at Cypress Point, circa 1929

36 x 48, oil on panel, originally painted: 1998 | Course: Cypress Point Club, Pebble Beach, California | Architects: Alister MacKenzie and Robert Hunter

Onset of Fall at Crystal Downs

36 x 48, oil on panel, 1998 | Course: Crystal Downs Country Club, Frankfort, Michigan | Architects: Alister MacKenzie and Perry Maxwell

ONSET OF FALL AT CRYSTAL DOWNS: *Located in northwest Michigan, Crystal Downs Country Club opened in 1931. The course was a collaboration between two of golf architecture's finest talents, Alister MacKenzie and Perry Maxwell. MacKenzie was literally duped into making the long journey into northern Michigan on his way back from a several-week stay at Augusta National. When MacKenzie finally arrived at the site, his frustration from having been misled gave way to amazement at the startling landscape that became Crystal Downs. He and Maxwell routed the course together but MacKenzie left the construction of his plans up to Maxwell, who he referred to as his "Midwest Associate." The result is one of golf's most original masterpieces, offering the ultimate in variety, naturalness, and strategy. Depicted here is the par-4 eighteenth, a 400-yard downhill, dogleg right that plays to a green at the base of two slopes. This view is from a path which players take back to a small golf clubhouse. Some walk this path with little regard for the lovely setting behind and below you, while others stop midway to take in this view of yet another beautifully crafted MacKenzie/Maxwell green complex.*

Several years after Crystal Downs opened and the Great Depression had set in, Perry Maxwell shared his thoughts on the evolution of golf course design and the overall American version of golf, an adaptation he had little regard for compared to the game played in Scotland:

"It is my theory that nature must precede the architect in the laying out of links. It is futile to attempt the transformation of wholly inadequate acres into an adequate course. Invariably the result is the inauguration of an earthquake. The site of a golf course should be there, not brought there...Many an acre of magnificent land has been utterly destroyed by the steam shovel, throwing up its billows of earth, biting out traps and bunkers, transposing landmarks that are contemporaries of Genesis...the majority of American golf clubs are in the red, gore of the stream shovel, blood drawn by mound builders. We have learned nothing from Scotland and England where the ancient and honorable game can be enjoyed on marvelous links at one tenth the admission fees, dues, green fees, etc., that prevail in the land of the free."

TENTH AT PINE VALLEY, CIRCA 1925: *George Crump may have fretted over the merits of this devilish 134-yard par 3. But 80 years after play began at Pine Valley, the tenth is one of golf's most beloved short one-shotters. This, despite the modern day view that penal short par 3s are not necessarily the best kind of one-shotter because they are often "unfair" to misplayed shots.*

Crump devoted his life to building Pine Valley after his wife of just one year passed away unexpectedly. He sold the family hotel, moved to the site and spent several years creating the course until his untimely death in January of 1918. Though he never played the completed course, Crump did see most of its design through the key construction stages. Golf great Chick Evans summarized the devoted artistry of Crump: "The Pine Valley course to a greater degree than any course I have ever seen possesses individuality. Everywhere this individuality was shown, nowhere more than on the greens, but Mr. Crump worked constantly on the whole landscape garden as if it were a picture, adding the needed touch here and there with the patience of an artist. It was pleasant to see the varicolored bushes that marked the line of play, which were but one of many refinements."

Note that in Mike Miller's depiction here, the front right "pot" bunker has begun to evolve. This bunker was not in Crump's original design. The bunker simply evolved and today is several feet deeper than its depiction here. The hazard has also earned a rather lewd name referred to by many a frustrated golfer who has fallen victim to this deep bunker. However, its role in lending drama and joyful interest to this hole cannot be overestimated.

Tenth at Pine Valley, circa 1925

48 x 36, oil on panel, 1998 | Course: Pine Valley Golf Club, Clementon, New Jersey | Architect: George Crump

Eleventh at Merion, circa 1997

48 x 36, oil on panel, 1998 | Course: Merion Golf Club, East Course, Ardmore, Pennsylvania | Architects: Hugh Wilson and William Flynn

ELEVENTH AT MERION, CIRCA 1997: *Depicted here in its modern state, the 369-yard, par-4 eleventh at Merion does not look much different than it did in September of 1930 when Bobby Jones closed out his final U.S. Amateur match to win the "Grand Slam." The tee shot here is blind and even a bit peculiar. If designed this way today, the architect would be chastised for not knocking down the hill that partially obstructs your view of the landing area. Thankfully, such a mind-set did not exist in Hugh Wilson's day. Wilson and William Flynn were not concerned with creating perfect visibility and they knew the golfers would soon learn how to play the tee shot. It's the approach here that is most special, perhaps one of the best in golf. Just a short iron is usually all that is needed, but the shot has frightened many great players due to the creek coming into play on the front right as well as to the rear. The back-left hole location is just as difficult to approach because of a well-placed bunker. The ancient-looking stone wall that supports the green combines with the irregular shape of the creek to make this green complex one of the game's masterpieces. Even though he was an amateur designer, Hugh Wilson was quite the student and artist. With help from William Flynn during the early '20s, they shaped Merion into one of the game's most important and influential designs.*

FALL AT CYPRESS POINT, SECOND GREEN, CIRCA 1929: *Alister MacKenzie and Robert Hunter's attractive second green at Cypress Point required a bit more "in the field" attention than others at this course. Most of the Cypress Point green sites were natural, but the second required subtle shaping and creativity to achieve its distinctive character. During construction the left-hand side of the green was elevated several feet above the existing ground, though it's hardly noticeable until you walk down a slope to the third tee. Depicted here in the early years when a dramatic "whale's tail" bay defined the left-front bunker, the second green is the conclusion to a long, dramatic dogleg-left, 550-yard, par 5. Set at the base of towering Monterey Pines, many observers have pointed out how MacKenzie, Hunter, and their talented American Golf Course Construction Company crew worked so carefully to mimic the lines of nature. In this case, the rugged, jagged edges of the bunkers seem to mimic the canopy of the pines. In Mike Miller's rendition of the second green complex, the loose style in which he presents the image emphasizes the complementary character of the bunker edges.*

In their timeless book The Architectural Side of Golf, *H.N. Wethered and Tom Simpson seemed to be describing the second green at Cypress Point when laying out their fundamentals for art in golf design: "A course should merge pleasantly into the landscape; the folds of greens and fairways should present agreeable curves against backgrounds of trees and hills; and where it is necessary to move earth to heighten levels or form depressions in new ground, the thing should be done with the delicacy of a sculptor modeling his clay."*

Fall at Cypress Point, Second Green, circa 1929

21 x 25, oil on panel, 1997 | Course: Cypress Point Club, Pebble Beach, California | Architects: Alister MacKenzie and Robert Hunter

No real lover of golf with artistic understanding would undertake to measure the quality or fascination of a golf hole by a yard-stick, any more than a critic of poetry would attempt to measure the supreme sentiment expressed in a poem by the same method. One can understand the meter, but one cannot measure the soul expressed. It is absolutely inconceivable.

C.B. MACDONALD

Genuine Variety

Whether it be in music, film, painting, or even golf architecture, variety is the element above any other that compels us to study various works of art. The variety of artistic expressions and styles adds zest to life and allows each of us to seek out art that suits our tastes. Yet in golf, the modern game seems determined to eliminate variety—to confine our choices to a select few aesthetic styles and even fewer types of routings or strategic possibilities. The aim would seem to be to make all courses look the same, and we know how fatal that would be for golf, no matter how fine the individual holes are.

We've read or heard it said many times: just like in life, variety is the spice of golf. It's the soul of the game. The variety of courses and ways to swing a club or attack a hole separates golf from all other sports.

Every old architect preached and pleaded that future golfers not lose sight of this all-important idea: That somehow, in some way, a distinct and original variety of courses signifies the ultimate artistic achievement in golf architecture. And they stated repeatedly that golf holes should be designed to give you multiple ways to play them in order to test one's mind, and to allow players of all levels to enjoy them. Simply put, they believed variety was the origin of "fun" golf and the key to long-term health of the game.

Yet why is creating variety in our designs becoming so difficult in contemporary golf? Why are we seeing less variety in course setups from day to day? How do architects spend millions on a design, producing holes that bear little distinction from the course they built down the street?

Because we have taken the vital concept of variety and thrown it out the window, only to see it in a newly redefined, resculpted, and transmogrified form known as *balance*.

But, you argue, how can variety be dead when no two courses and no two golf holes are *exactly* alike regardless of the era they were constructed? Or that no two days on a course are *exactly* alike?

It is a fair question, but we are talking about *genuine* variety. Not what the scorecard tells us a particular course has to offer in the way of a balanced set of par 3s, par 4s, and par 5s. No, the kind of genuine variety that presents an uncontrived mix of shots, looks and emotions evoked by the design.

The death of honest variety never really dawned on me until I obtained a yearly newsletter of an elite magazine's course-ranking panel. The newsletter contains panelist comments on all of the year's best new courses and the various nominees that were unable to win one of the magazine's awards.

Now, I applaud the panel's attempts to analyze many facets of architecture and to ask their panelists to dig deep into the nuances of a course. And their desire to identify variety is wonderful. Unfortunately, the criterion has the panel looking at architecture in a strange way and unintentionally misunderstanding variety.

As if they were storeroom clerks assigned with a clipboard doing inventory, the modern day panelist has been asked to use their ballot to mark off each dogleg right, each straight hole, and the yardages of the various holes. Then they comment about the course's variety based on whether it had a balanced variety of holes. If it did, then it called upon the misunderstood, trite, "every shot in the bag." Again, the intentions are virtuous, but the diligence with which they do their work has led to an overemphasis on balance as opposed to honest variety.

In the newsletter the panelists often mentioned that a course had a preponderance of dogleg lefts or an unbalanced set of par-5 distances. Or that the par 3s called upon only slightly similar shots. Thus, a course lost hefty points when judging variety because a proper balance was not offered.

However, if a course called on "every club in the bag" during the panelist's lone go-around, it earned high marks regardless of whether the holes were thought-provoking or fun to play. If the scorecard indicated a proper balance of par-36 per nine and counterweighted yardages, then variety appeared to exist. If a certain prescribed and balanced set of par 4s was not prevalent, say two short ones, four medium length holes, and four long ones, the variety was off-kilter.

Variety is so much more than a mere examination of the numbers to determine if all the stock is on hand. A golf course's singular character stems from the charisma of each hole and how each fits the pieces of the 18-hole puzzle. If the land genuinely dictates how the holes are laid out and played, as most modern architects claim, then the chances of reaching the various balanced "norms" in design will be difficult unless the architect uses a bulldozer to rearrange the terrain (which is often the case). Only on dead flat property can the architect provide two uniformly balanced nines of par-36, with two par 3s and two par 5s per nine and the "proper" yardage symmetry. Assuming the land is respected or its subtle features even noticed by the architect, any property with even the slightest bit of topography will surely throw in some wrinkle that prevents this perfect balance. Unless, of course, the architect disregards his subject matter and rearranges the canvas to his liking. After reading how the panelists examine a golf course from this perspective of "variety," you can understand why award-starved architects rearrange the land to conform to what has become accepted as the norm: par-72, 7,000 yards, two par 5s per nine and four par 3s of varying lengths.

Pebble Beach Golf Links, with its two par 5s and two par 3s per nine looks balanced on the scorecard. In reality it is much more original, natural, and fascinating than what the numbers tell us, and no golfer has ever left there feeling like they didn't have a full examination of their skills.

Pebble Beach starts off with several simple holes, and then turns tough all the way to the end, with a particularly difficult stretch of golf on holes eight through ten. The nines are not balanced nor is this a textbook way to present a course, yet it flows wonderfully and in an original, distinctive way. No two holes even remotely play or feel the same, and if the gentle start is not taken advantage of, even more pressure is added to the awaiting ocean holes. All of this lends authentic variety to Pebble Beach.

Like anyone initially interested in golf architecture, my first experience in genuine variety came after seeing enough courses with different bunker and green complex styles to know that the possibilities of recreating interesting golf are endless. As evidenced by the variety of par 3s featured in this chapter, holes can come in a variety of shapes and sizes with a divergence of bunker looks and a multitude of playing options. In other words, different artistic styles lend variety to architecture, but the handiwork of the architect can never genuinely capture the ultimate in variety that is provided when taking advantage of natural features.

After spending time walking a property and helping with the development of a routing on a lovely but environmentally restricted piece of land, I came to the realization that the genuine variety found in timeless designs is created by something the architect has little control over. Something which the wise architect always seeks out, obeys once he finds it, and uses to his advantage: the contours and features provided by Mother Nature.

Whether it be Cypress Point, Pine Valley, Crystal Downs, Pebble Beach, Sand Hills, or lesser-known gems like Fisher's Island and Baltimore Country Club, unique designs fit their property. After finding the finest features and creating a mix of holes by taking advantage of the land, the talented architect complements his natural "discoveries" with features that will augment everyday play. If the architect genuinely followed the terrain in routing the holes (and we assume that the ground offered some combination of ridges, swales, or hazards), then the course will take on its own distinct character. Genuine variety will be found and most likely, the layout will not fit the expected norms of a ranking panelist. It may have too many dogleg lefts or one too many uphill holes, but in all likelihood most of the holes will have plenty of charm and memorability because of nature's distinctive, sometimes quirky design input.

Variety, in other words, is a subtle feature. It can't be detected by analyzing a scorecard, like one might pour over a spreadsheet. Just as one cannot measure the beauty of a melody with some sort of mathematic scale, or try to compute the emotional power of a film by perusing a checklist to determine if the director followed textbook filmmaking guidelines.

In golf architecture, determining variety by whether or not the player used every club in his bag on a one-round evaluation is just as ludicrous. Besides, on bad days we all use every club in our bag at some point because we're taking so many shots.

Genuine variety requires time absorbing the canvas before you. An appreciation of nature's ability to utilize the best contours and natural hazards is also necessary. But these nuances cannot be fully appreciated by playing a course once or twice, just as an ingenious symphony or a powerful film cannot be genuinely appreciated if experienced only once. And those layouts that charm us over time are those where we learn and appreciate subtle features during repeat visits. Almost always, those little nooks and crannies that lend so much to our discoveries were derived from natural features.

Many renowned designs look flawed if we judge them by the scorecard or the architect's schematic rendering, while many layouts with little in the way of interesting possibilities look outstanding on paper.

I can say with little hesitation that the golf course routing that I helped to create has serious "balance" problems when looking at the scorecard or even at the sequence of holes on paper. The front nine has three par 5s and three par 3s. There is only one long par 4 on the front, with two very short par 4s on that same nine. Four of the course's five three-shotters travel in roughly the same direction, including two back-to-back par 5s at holes nine and ten. Yet before the ground is even cleared, I know each hole will be distinctive simply because of the contours, the existing hazards, and the playing directions which will meet the prevailing wind at slightly different angles.

Meanwhile, the incoming nine provides a more "balanced" set that largely conforms to the expected norms on paper, though the actual holes themselves figure to have plenty of original character thanks to both subtle and some dramatic natural features. These holes will offer up a distinctive variety of shots because the terrain is so unique to each hole, and for that matter, to any other holes I can recall.

So why is the front nine I describe flawed in the modern day definition of variety? Because we fit the holes to the land and worked around environmentally sensitive areas. The front nine is much shorter than the back, always a no-no in the "balance" mind-set. But the variety experienced by the golfers will prove singular because the holes will be distinctive and fun, and each will be unlike any other on the course. That's because the land is allowed to shape them and lend the variety. We are merely throwing in a few touches to spice things up

strategically or aesthetically, but those additions are minor compared to the unmatched character created long before anyone ever set foot on the property.

Assuming an architect has taken advantage of natural features on a site, golfers sense and appreciate the kind of genuine variety accentuated by the architect because man never has, and never will be able to replicate what nature has to offer. If a semiblind shot exists because of an exisiting hill, golfers do learn to accept it and adapt. But if the blindness was artificially created, it never takes on much charm and is usually found to be more obnoxious than interesting.

And therein lies the problem as to why so much modern day design is lacking artistry that should be more prevalent. Man often believes he can be as good or better than nature. He feels he can rearrange the land to better suit his needs. Yet how many rearranged courses genuinely feel good or look beautiful? How many of those furnish the ultimate natural golf "experience" that a Crystal Downs or a Cypress Point can provide—two courses, which, besides being highly ranked and nearly perfect, might be considered extremely unusual on paper because they don't conform to the modern day "norms" of golf architecture.

At the expense of artistry in golf architecture, conformity and balance have prevailed. The topography and the character of land now come second to what is perceived as the best kind of golf: par-72, "championship" yardage and proportionately weighted nines.

It's a bit like Mike Miller trying to use the same size canvas and a predetermined group of colors for each golf landscape he paints. If he were to approach his paintings this way regardless of the subject matter, the time of day, or the season, there would not be much reason to keep turning the pages. The result would be a banality similar to that found in balance-driven golf course design.

All too often, the modern golf architect forces what he and the average golfer perceive as the most balanced subject matter on canvases ill-suited to such golf holes. They force colors (golf holes) onto their canvas (terrain) that do not fit. If the land doesn't conform to what the architect thinks is best for that point in the round, he simply rearranges the land to fit the piece of the "balance" puzzle he's looking for. Yet when that kind of rearrangement and disfigurement of nature occurs, genuine variety and charm are lost.

There are certain golf architects practicing today who can genuinely let the land dictate the design, just as there are artists who let the subject matter determine the size of the canvas or the tonality of the painting. There is a breed of modern golf architect who looks at the subject, studies it in different lights, different winds, and different seasons, and figures out how to approach the subject with the appropriate colors and style. They find the contours and natural features that work best and design their hole in such a way that they take advantage of those elements or even subtly accentuate them. And if during construction they find a better alternative to what they initially planned, they make the adjustment for the long-term good of the course, even if it means admitting their initial perceptions were wrong. The resulting layouts are rare examples of original modern design, but were a daily occurrence in classic 1920's golf architecture.

There is even genuine variety to be found in the architecture of Charles Blair Macdonald and Seth Raynor, who took certain design concepts (Redan, Eden, and Biarritz holes)

and built them over and over again. How did they achieve honest, interesting variety while stamping certain concepts onto the land?

They found topography suited to those ideas, and then worked a Redan or an Eden into the land while accentuating what existed before they arrived. Thus, even their imported concepts took on a flair of originality because they never forced them onto the property, but instead, let the terrain call out for a certain type of hole. And thus, Macdonald and Raynor maintained a subtle variety in their hole "concept" that remains fresh even today.

So is genuine variety really as simple as allowing nature to dictate the design? Does it only require an architect to route the property on foot and make subtle adjustments as construction progresses? Is it a matter of finding the best features, designing around them or even accentuating them, even if it means throwing balanced nines or 7,000 yard plateaus out the window? Absolutely.

Fresh, original, and unforced variety in golf course design starts with the architect.

However, the kind of surprising, but always interesting variety can only become commonplace with acceptance from the everyday golfer and the people who dream up and finance golf course projects. Instead of judging golf design by the numbers on the card or the map on the planner's desk, the golfer must understand that true architectural variety must stem from the topography. They must allow architects to utilize the features nature has left us for the betterment of their golf.

Then, and only then, can the architect take golf design to new and original places.

The Architect's Canvas and Colors

BY MAX BEHR, 1928

The object of golf architecture is to give an intelligent purpose to the striking of a golf ball. To be worthwhile, this purpose must excite and hold interest. If it fails in this, the character of the architecture is at fault.

This permits us by analogy to compare the work of the golf architect with that of the painter. The architect's canvas, like the painter's, is made up of the dimension's length and width: his colors are his hazards, the various kinds and degrees of physical difficulties presented. These difficulties are either some impediment to the clubhead in striking the ball or a restriction upon the manner in which it must be played to overcome some future obstacle. On the dark side, they begin with the black of an unplayable lie, and gradually grow lighter through water, blindness, bunkers, trees, long grass, hills and hollows, until, with a gentle slope, they disappear in the white of a perfect lie.

However, unlike the painter, rarely does the architect have a clean canvas to work on. To a greater or lesser extent the ground already has character; that is color. Golf architecture depends on the manner and style in which the existing character of the ground is interpreted and modified.

We shall better understand the manner in which hazards should be employed if we imagine a course laid out on dead level turf. In other words, a canvas to which no color has been applied. Play on such a course would be monotonous. It is also evident that, to the expert, it would be as difficult as for the inexpert. What then, should the function of hazards be? The answer is: to attack skill through the mind.

This hazards can do only when they have the power to excite our interest. A real interest may be defined as "an identification of ourselves with something that is real independently of us." Hazards used to penalize errors of skill are the opposite of this as their only reason for existence is wholly dependent upon our errors. Therefore, hazards in such a relation serve no intelligent purpose.

What do we mean by "intelligent purpose?"

This becomes apparent when we carry our analogy further and understand the use to which the artist puts his colors. Needless to say, he does not employ them separately to express the particular and original character of each. On the contrary, the artist combines his colors in certain relations. From these relations ideas emerge. Hence the colors lose their identity in becoming part of a greater whole. Just so, hazards cannot be used solely to express their color of penalty, for when they become part of a greater whole, they lose their identity as penalty. Serving to express their ideas, they become associated with thought, and their concern with the ball is necessarily secondary.

From the standpoint of art this renders meaningless all attempts to standardize the dimensions of the parts of a golf hole. For instance, there is no such thing as an arbitrary size of greens for holes of various length. This is merely the use of dimension as penalty, the tendency of which is to encourage slugging. The nearer the ball can be driven to the hole, the less dimension imposes its penalty, and mere brawn is thus given too great an advantage over precise skill. Golf architecture is not a science. Creatively it is not amenable to measurable knowledge.

The failure to understand this is one reason responsible for the dilemma in the minds of most golfers who try to come to a logical understanding of golf architecture and get nowhere.

Golf architecture, if it is to have a lasting appeal, must do justice to all players, and this it can do only when hazards are used in the strategic form. Art is freedom, therefore art is the only means by which we can insure a feeling of freedom to the golfer. Diminish freedom by discipline, and the joy in accomplishment depreciates; but as golf has no other justification for existence than to heighten the joy of living, to diminish this is to defeat the purpose of golf. It follows that the use of penalty to the end of restricting, disciplining and thus magnifying the expression of instinct is not golf architecture. It weakens rather than strengthens.

Thus we see that golf architecture, because it is an art, has to do with furthering the amenities of life. But when so-called architecture only contributes to its trials and tribulations, it loses both the sense and the dignity of its calling. And, as an art, it is first of all a skill only in the degree to which skill falls short of the undertakings the mind has set it. It should never impose its will upon the golfer. Its form should invite the golfer to impose his will upon it.

AFTER A STORM, FOURTH AT BALTIMORE, CIRCA 1929: *This mid-length par 3 of 163 yards starts from an elevated tee and plays to an enormous sloping green. Though simple in appearance, the shot is an exciting one because of the menacing front bunkers, which are much deeper than they appear here. The green has numerous hole location possibilities, which adds to the variety presented by A.W. Tillinghast. He was a strong believer in creating holes that were memorable without being overdone. The fourth at Baltimore is a hole that no one forgets after seeing this fine layout, and yet it is just one of eighteen sound holes on the East Course.*

Tillinghast best summed up his philosophy on golf architecture when he wrote:

"A round of golf should present eighteen inspirations—not necessarily thrills, for spectacular holes may be sadly overdone. Every hole may be constructed to provide charm without being obtrusive with it. When I speak of a hole being inspiring, it is not intended to infer that the visitor is to be subject to attacks of hysteria on every teeing ground as he casts his eye over the fairway to the green for the first time, and to be so overwhelmed with the outstanding features, both natural and manufactured, that he can not keep his eye on the ball. It must be remembered that the great majority of golfers are aiming to reduce their previous best performance by five strokes if possible, first, last, and all the time, and if any one of them arrives at the home teeing ground with this possibility in reach, he is not caring two hoots whether he is driving off from nearby an ancient oak of majestic size and form or a dead sassafras. If his round ends happily it is one beautiful course. Such is human nature."

After a Storm, Fourth at Baltimore, circa 1929

12 x 24, oil on panel, 1998 | Course: Baltimore Country Club, East Course, Baltimore, Maryland | Architect: A.W. Tillinghast

The Sandy Carry on Pine Valley's Third

36 x 48, oil on panel, 1999 | Course: Pine Valley Golf Club, Clementon, New Jersey | Architect: George Crump

THE SANDY CARRY ON PINE VALLEY'S THIRD: *This classic 181-yard, par 3 is depicted by Miller in the 1930s when the pines were taller than in Crump's day. Though often referred to as somewhat of a "Redan" type par 3, the third at Pine Valley has a distinct character of its own. The shot requires a courageous right-to-left play in order to land your approach near the back-left hole locations. However, most players are pleased just to land on this putting surface and have a chance at two-putting for a par. The shaping of this green, the irregular edges of the hazard banks, and the bunkering immediately surrounding the putting surface are some of the finest man-made creations ever seen in golf.*

Robert Hunter once summed up a course with the ultimate in variety, and his words seem to capture the essence of Pine Valley where the variety of holes and looks presented by George Crump are as distinct as any course in the world. Hunter wrote, "Really good golf holes are full of surprises, each one a bit better than the last. Like a first rate dinner, as soon as you have finished one course with beaming satisfaction something even better is placed before you. To arouse this zest each hole should have a character of its own. Its physiognomy should be quite distinct from that of its neighbors, and it should be one not easy to forget. Its personality should awaken your interest and cause you to question how best to approach it. It should present some problem to you in vivid form, and, even though that problem may be solved in two or three ways, it should be quite clear from the beginning that a choice must be made."

PASSING WEATHER, SEVENTEENTH AT SAND HILLS: *Opened in 1995, Sand Hills not only proves that a special course can be built inexpensively, but that it can be done with great care and artistry in this day of assembly-line courses. Two years were spent planning the course and crafting the hazards which make this design so unique. Ironically, Crenshaw had clipped and saved* Southwest Art *magazine photos of the Nebraska Sand Hills region many years before he was contacted regarding the chance to create a course in this remote location.*

The seventeenth is a short but exciting one-shotter. The view depicted by Miller is from the members' tee, an enjoyable pitch shot of around 100 yards. Another tee makes the hole play just slightly uphill, 146 yards away and to the right of this view. The green itself is tiny, but the hazards make this hole and Sand Hills so special. Crenshaw described the creation of the Sand Hills bunkering:

"The weather is harsh there, so they're going to constantly evolve. We agreed amongst ourselves that this was sort of a vast experiment. To us, it was way too early to go in there and start sod walling the bunkers or turfing them over because we wanted to see how they would evolve. Some of it was so good in its native form that we asked ourselves, 'how can you touch that?' Dave Axland [shaper] was tremendous in the way he devised the entire plan, where he would cut something out and if he didn't like it he'd just go get a chunk of native grass and replace it and let it heal on its own. He did it sparingly, but that got the texture and dimension of the little movements and the jaggedness just right."

Passing Weather, Seventeenth at Sand Hills

36 x 48, oil on panel, 1998 | Course: Sand Hills Golf Club, Mullen, Nebraska | Architects: Bill Coore and Ben Crenshaw

Passing Thunderstorm, Sixteenth at Fisher's Island

36 x 48, oil on panel, 1997 | Course: Fisher's Island Golf Club, Fisher's Island, New York | Architect: Seth Raynor

PASSING THUNDERSTORM, SIXTEENTH AT FISHER'S ISLAND: *This is the "Short" hole, a par 3 of 146 yards, one of many concept holes used in each of Raynor's designs. And though the "concept" may seem forced and perhaps even insulting to the original ideas of other architects, Raynor managed to fit the various renditions of these holes in naturally. He also added a different twist to each rendition of the Short. Even though the "Redan" and "Biarritz" have become the most popular concept holes to see at each of his courses, the "Short" is possibly the most fun for all players to tackle. The Short originated at The National Golf Links where Raynor's mentor C.B. Macdonald created a dramatic forced-carry short hole on the par-3 sixth.*

Macdonald, who battled many critics in his quest to reproduce sound design concepts from overseas in an attempt to educate golfers, wrote eloquently on the subject of variety: "There are many moot questions argued by noted designers of golf courses. The character and placing of hazards has always been a bone of contention. Why I cannot understand, because one has only to study the great holes that the world conceded are unexcelled. There should be every variety of hazards. Variety is not only 'the spice of life' but it is the very foundation of golfing architecture. Diversity in nature is universal. Let your golfing architecture mirror it. An ideal or classical golf course demands variety, personality, and, above all, the charm of romance."

SUMMER DAY AT PINEHURST, CIRCA 1935: *This classic 162-yard par 3 captures the essence of variety thanks to the number of hole locations this wonder of a green offers and the manner in which the hole can provide so many differently shaped shots. After the carry over the pine needles and unmaintained sandy area, the elevated green features a sharp fronting tier that guards the lower hole location. Another ridge separates the upper and lower halves with bunkers all around to add to the player's list of elements to consider. The variety of shots possible here is rather remarkable for a par 3. The one-shotter is the hardest hole for architects to create a multitude of strategies and shotmaking possibilities, yet Ross was a master at creating greens that would allow for such variety.*

Pinehurst's ninth, like so many of Ross's holes, is summed up succinctly by the great Scottish designer, who lived at Pinehurst and tinkered with this masterpiece for nearly 40 years:

"The golf holes on the best links in Scotland and England have several different ways of playing them, and because they do not present just one and only one way to everybody, the interest in the game increases with the diversity of its problems."

Summer Day at Pinehurst, circa 1935

36 x 48, oil on panel, 2000 | Course: Pinehurst Country Club, Course #2, Pinehurst, North Carolina | Architect: Donald Ross

SUNDOWN AT WINGED FOOT'S TENTH, CIRCA 1927: *Winged Foot's 190-yard, par-3 tenth provides one of golf's most famous shots and was considered by A.W. Tillinghast to be "the best par-3" he ever built. From a tee slightly elevated above the green, the player looks down on this well-bunkered green. Miller has illustrated the hole from the view of a golfer walking to the green, giving some sense of the massive scale of the bunkers and green complex. The Winged Foot terrain is relatively level, so to create these features and build them with a somewhat natural appearance, a great deal of fill was used and talented shapers did some of their finest work here for Tillinghast. The bunkers look remarkably similar today; however, Tillinghast's original putting surface has evolved into a smaller green than as depicted here in its late 1920s.*

Winged Foot is often criticized because of a perceived lack of variety, with many of the par-4s seemingly similar in length and challenge. However, this is more likely a result of the layout's overabundance of trees masking the individual character of each hole, instead of a faulty design by Tillinghast. Thankfully, Winged Foot has recently removed many trees and reinvigorated one of the best examples of "genuine" and subtle variety. Much of the East Course's diversity is based on the character of the greens, arguably as stern and interesting as any set you will find in golf.

Tillinghast, perhaps aware that the subtle range of green designs would be lost on some, wrote of Winged Foot: "As the various holes came to life they were of a sturdy breed. The contouring of the greens places a premium on the placement of drives, but never is there the necessity of facing a prodigious carry of the sink or swim sort. It is only the knowledge that the next shot must be played with rifle accuracy that brings the realization that the drive must be placed. The holes are like men, all rather similar from foot to neck, but with the greens showing the same varying characters as human faces."

Sundown at Winged Foot's Tenth, circa 1927

36 x 48, oil on panel, 2001 |Course: Winged Foot Golf Club, East Course, Mamaroneck, New York |Architect: A.W. Tillinghast

All men are tempted. There is no man that lives that can't be broken down, provided it is the right temptation, put in the right spot.

HENRY WARD BEECHER

The true hazard should draw the player towards it, should invite the golfer to come as near as he dare to the fire without burning his fingers. The man who can afford to take risks is the man who should gain the advantage.

JOHN LOW

Temptation

It has become commonplace in modern times to condense life-governing principles into lists, rankings or one-word descriptions. Yet few elements of genuine substance could ever be whittled down into such fragmented offerings, especially with regard to a pursuit as complex and mystifying as golf. However, even in our attempts throughout this book to discuss the art form better known as golf architecture, one word seemingly captures the most consistent element of enduring and amusing course design: temptation.

Temptation seduces us into trying specific shots and intrigues us when the surroundings cannot be classified as "pretty." Memorable, satisfying, and joyful shots are not merely those played in the most beautiful settings. They are largely the result of beguiling hole designs that offer tempting options.

As with any special work of art, there is an alluring quality to great holes—an element within their design that entices our imagination and inspires us to try a shot we had never before imagined. In golf architecture, the presentation of tempting choices, more than any other quality, attracts golfers to certain holes time and time again.

Do you feel a sense of urgency to play a long, straight hole lined with rough, trees, and no decisions to make? Does its flat green, with a systematically placed bunker left and a bunker right, captivate the senses? Does such a scenario give us the chance to imagine many creative shots that tempt us to try something out of character in order to obtain some reward?

Of course not.

The holes that we yearn to play repeatedly are those that prompt us to try something of which we may or may not be capable. They appeal on repeat visits no matter how much trauma they have caused us in the past because they require that decisions be made in order to conquer them. Along with an appealing choice to make, they motivate us to overcome our fears and pull off our best shot, even if common sense tells us a wise layup and a solid wedge shot will give us a safe, acceptable result.

Temptation is the reason it's fun to play to a well-conceived short par 3—the kind with a hole location perched precariously on a hazard-surrounded peninsula, with a safe outlet that can easily be hit but which doesn't test the golfer's courage. The intriguing prospect of going straight at the hole and making a heroic birdie is the shot we might remember for years. If we can pull it off.

And if we don't, the thrill of trying is still far more satisfying than playing a series of holes that merely ask us to obey dull situations.

Every course should have two short par 4s in order to present as much temptation as possible. Players of all levels can enjoy the options available to us on short two-shotters. Everyone can be tempted into trying something more than they are perhaps capable of by a short par 4. The best player in the world can fall victim to short par-4 temptation when presented with a healthy equilibrium of safe choices combined with the well-conceived, seductive option of driving the green. And the shorter hitters can sneak up and snatch par or birdie if they attack the hole with wisdom.

Temptation is the reason par 5s that are reachable in two shots—as opposed to the expected three—are the most enjoyable holes of all if they present options where a legitimate reward is dangled in front of the spellbound player. They dupe everyone into having a go at the hole in one less shot than normal, and their paltry yardage prompts us to believe that the architect is giving us the opportunity to make birdie and compensate for earlier indiscretions. Again, the beauty of shrewdly designed reachable par 5 is the wise player's ability to make up for a lack of power with wise play that can beat the reckless player.

Yet temptation, the best kind anyway, is consistently missing from modern day golf course design. The Cypress Points and Augusta Nationals of the world do not present merely one tempting decision on a single "signature" hole designated as the most photogenic. In this day when courses are resigned to having one "signature" hole featuring one heroic shot, the classic courses present tempting shots throughout, with seductive decisions to be made every step of the way. And on occasion they present temptation that is so grueling and tantalizing that the hole's power can be felt long before the player even reaches its tee.

For those who love the sporting aspect of golf, it is disheartening to see this transformation in design away from tempting holes and a shift toward most golf only asking us to obey and avoid trouble. This situation is made even more frustrating because the architect can execute the creation of beguiling designs with relatively little effort.

To produce temptation in design, the architect must take time sculpting his design "in the field" both prior to and during construction. Perfecting tee, green, and bunker placement, while finding contours and other natural features to obtain the optimum sporting hole, are the elements that give birth to tempting choices. Creating enticing shots is an art form, requiring patience and care as the course is built.

The creation of lasting and interesting design also requires that the architect be given the canvas he needs to explore possibilities. This is often *not* the case as developers understandably keep the best land for housing, or environmentalists protect natural resources. Still, the creative architect can find positive features in most sites. But the architect needs some leeway from the golfer to pursue originality in their routing and hole designs. He must be given the freedom to set aside conventional norms in order to discover the best potential golf holes.

If the architect can find the acreage that gives the player enough space to play carefully while also presenting a more enticing option, the doors to temptation are opened. Room to choose provides the player with alternative routes to take, prompting the golfer to consider pulling off heroic shots even when there is a safe haven that is clearly the "logical" way to go.

Modern American design, however, views wide fairways as a negative design element or simply refuses to allow architects enough acreage to have proper width. The desire to reach 7,000 yards often consumes acreage that would have been better served for wider playing corridors. But the disappearance of width is not simply relegated to fairways.

"Ideal" greens in modern design are thought to be smallish targets because that's what golfers find on many classic designs. But old photographs are showing that the master architects created much larger greens than we see today and many clubs are in the process of restoring putting surfaces to their original size. Though small greens work in some situations, fewer hole location options present nightmares for maintenance. Worse, smaller greens mean few alternatives for the kind of variety that leads to genuinely tempting golf.

Pick any of the undisputed "great" holes in golf, and at their core is the element of temptation. Most of the great ones are beautiful. But, it is their ability to seduce us to try for something bold, something courageous, while leaving room to play safely for the golfer with less courage.

The par-3 sixteenth at Cypress Point plays over the Pacific Ocean with the wind blowing in off the sea. Sure, it is a very "difficult" hole to par. But it is the temptation to play over the Pacific Ocean and at the green, even with a large left-hand bailout area, that is the genius of this hole. The temptation is so great that its architect, Alister MacKenzie, deemed it "the

Lindbergh Thrill." The heroic possibility of launching your shot over a huge body of water with the triumphant reward of landing safely on the other side is the ultimate thrill in golf. To play a shot over such a natural chasm and to carry it off is an experience every golfer remembers throughout his golfing life.

The par-5 thirteenth hole at Augusta National is a paltry 465 yards from the members' tees, and yet it teases and tortures great players more than any hole in the world. A player on his game believes a score of five is a letdown because birdie or even eagle is always within reach. It beguiles you into cutting off that creek-and-pine-guarded corner, allowing for a short club to be used to attack the putting surface that is perched above the trickling stream. And even if you are further from the green than you want to be, the lack of water in the creek and its meager size tempts you to try anyway, because a miss might just get lucky and end up on a sand bar, or better, miss the creek altogether.

So many possibilities, so many tempting choices.

The most perplexing par 4 in golf is the Road Hole at St. Andrews, the seventeenth. It starts with a peculiar blind drive over a green shed the size of an average American home. This is the route to go if you want to reach the green in two shots. However, there is out-of-bounds along the right that can't be seen. But we all know the boundary is there, thanks to the annoying hotel that now sits where the railway station used to be. The slim shape of the Road Hole green and its angle in relation to the fairway makes playing down the right-hand side more tempting. The safe play left of the green shed will probably leave you laying up and playing the hole as a par 5, or at best, having a longer and more difficult shot to the right side of the putting surface. The disastrous Road Hole bunker guards the left side hole locations while the right side sits open with a sharp tier to deal with. But a generous safe zone below the tier awaits the safe and often shrewd play.

To the immediate rear of the green is the infamous road from which the hole earns its less than flattering name. Balls finding the pavement or the area beyond the road will meet an almost certain disastrous end. The safe play is to hit your approach well short (in the neighborhood of the lower green tier). But temptation tells you that with only one more hole to play, a much-needed four can best be obtained by hitting directly to the top level, but at the risk of hitting over and onto the road. It is the most testing and mind-boggling of all shots in golf, and every golfing great has been tempted by the Road Hole and its fascinating possibilities.

To inject tempting shots into design, the architect must also have more than "room" with which to present options. Tantalizing holes require the architect to take chances by utilizing hazards of all sorts, including ground contours and the implementation of engaging putting surface contours that help dictate how the hole is attacked. The golfer must accept that grueling decisions and an occasional unfair bounce will enter into this equation. They also must concur that greens need contours—even at the expense of speed—in order to create interesting golf. In order to have the privilege of playing exceptional golf holes, that which seems fair or straightforward might have to be sacrificed now and then. After all, this is a sport right? It's not life or death, is it? Our scores and the equity with which we are treated on a golf course should not have an impact on the things that really matter, should they?

The modern mind-set in golf has placed an emphasis on fairness and perfect visibility of all hazards, and praises holes that play down narrow corridors because they are "tough to par." These "either/or" expectations for golf holes were less prevalent during the "Golden Age" when the Crystal Downs, Cypress Points, Rivieras, Merions, and Pinehursts of the world were created. And if fairness was ever a mandate from the developer to, say, Alister MacKenzie, he and his counterparts were artistically deft enough to ensure that the holes balanced risk and reward. But today we live in an era when the touring professionals' pleas for fairness are heeded and even considered the last word on design. Yet rarely are touring professionals' views on golf architecture worthwhile because they are almost never looking out for the best interests of golf. Remember, these are people trying to make their living on golf courses. Naturally they will want every design element to be as straightforward as can be.

There is an art to imagining, creating, and ultimately deciding to carry out a certain shot. Whether it be a bump and run seven-iron or a slicing four-wood from 200 yards out, the joy of envisioning and carrying out such heroic shots is what golfers ultimately remember over their mostly indifferent shots. Incomparable joy comes when we fret over which option to take, only to look back and see that the decision made was the best one when we pulled it off with creative shotmaking. Satisfaction even comes with failure, because we have little doubt that we did our best and only failed in accomplishing something heroic.

The rare mixture of our best effort overcoming the most tempting choice the architect can offer brings more satisfaction than any other element in golf. Overcoming fear and doubt is what great golf and the timeless courses are all about. It's why some holes will keep enduring and why so many less daring, less varied, less inspirational, and ultimately less tempting designs will long be forgotten.

The Correct Use of Penalty

BY MAX BEHR, 1926

Hazards are not penal areas. Punishment is not the end that penalty serves. On the contrary, hazards are pressure areas acting upon the mind. They make a call upon intelligence. And intelligence, in terms of pastimes, may be defined as the skill of the mind to cope with experience. Therefore if a golf hole is to have form, its hazards must so react upon one another as to create unity. And as a result of unity the mind of the player is projected into the future. Each stroke comprehends not only an immediate problem but a future problem as well. It follows that every hazard of a hole, even the bunkers that abut upon the green of a three-shot hole, must be felt by the player at the tee. Thus the golfer, just as the player of games, is forced to assume immediate risks if he wishes to rid himself of future liabilities.

In this respect penal holes mean nothing. The confinement of width of play by the rough precludes to a great extent the creating of future threats. Therefore the penal idea that makes a virtue of rough with its penal bunkers robs nature, the opponent, of deploying herself strategically. And that simply means intelligently. And whenever we curtail anything so that it cannot fully express itself, inhibitions are setup and degeneration sets in. That delicate and subtle relation of values that make things worthwhile is broken down. False values are set up. And these are always quantity values.

The golf architect, therefore, is not at all concerned with chastising faulty strokes. It is his business to arrange a field of play so as to stimulate interest. And interest "implies concern, not with ourselves, but with something that is real independently of us." And that is exactly what a penal bunker is not. It is a reality that stands in relation to us; something provided for our special benefit. It does not exist to protect the hole, something real independent of us and which we are most concerned to play out ball into, but exists merely as a mirror of our faults. Thus the penal school puts the cart before the horse. And the golfer instead of pitting his skill against an intelligent opposition of hazards is driven to a battle with himself. This means an absolute negation of interest. And the reason why most golfers stand for it is simply because they still are at that stage where there principle concern is hitting the ball. They are learning to walk, and pat themselves on the back when their balls do not slip into the gutter of the rough. But I think it will always be found that the holes golfers are most proud of on their home courses are those which contain an element of strategy.

The concern of the architect, therefore, should be positive and have solely to do with what the golfer should do. His mission is not that of a moralist, the principal word of whose vocabulary is DON'T. The golfer should not be made to feel that he must renounce, that the primary object for him is to conquer his faults. It is not the architect to inform him when he has played badly. That is the province of his professional. No, the mission of the architect is that of a leader. By the deployment of his hazards he exhorts the golfer to do his best, enticing him at times "to shoot the bones for the whole works." Thus he instills in the golfer a spirit of conquest by presenting him with definite objectives upon which he must concentrate. It is for the golfer to stamp his law upon the ground. It is in no way the business of the architect to stamp his law upon the golfer. But thus it is in most cases. The penal school of golf spells death to that spirit of independence, life and freedom which we are all seeking, and which we should find of all places in our recreations.

SIXTEENTH AT CYPRESS POINT, CIRCA 1929: *Easily the most photographed hole in golf, Cypress Point's sixteenth also presents the game's most tempting shot. As Clint Eastwood's Detective Harry Calahan might offer in summing up this hole, "a man has got to know his limitations." And stepping onto this tee, golfers are confronted with the temptation to ignore their shortcomings in an attempt to achieve the ultimate thrill of landing a tee shot onto this green.*

Captured here on a calm summer day and viewed from above the path that players take after teeing off, the sixteenth looks rather benign in this version by Miller. But at 233 yards and playing over the Pacific, it is anything but simple. The problems are often compounded by the fact that anyone who plays this hole only once or twice can't resist the temptation to go for the green, even if one of Cypress Point's wise caddies is telling you to play safely. As Robert Hunter once wrote, "The temptation to bite off more and more, as one improves in play, is the best possible incentive to better golf." And no hole in golf provides more incentive to try pulling off your best shot by inching as close to the green as possible. No par 3 in golf matches the tempting qualities of Cypress Point's sixteenth.

The story of how this hole came to be such a famous one-shotter is well known but worth repeating. MacKenzie passed the story along in several articles and his book, The Spirit of St. Andrews:

"To give honor where it is due, I must say that, except for minor details in construction, I was in no way responsible for the hole. It was largely due to the vision of Miss Marion Hollins. It was suggested to her by the late Seth Raynor that it was a pity the carry over the ocean was too long to enable a hole to be designed on this particular site. Miss Hollins said she did not think it was an impossible carry. She then teed up a ball and drove to the middle of the site for the suggested green. There are three alternative routes, namely, the direct route over 200 yards of ocean to the green, an intermediate route over about 100 yards of ocean, and a still shorter route to the left. A well played shot to the lone Cypress tree with a nicely calculated slice gets the help of the slope and runs very near the green, enabling the player to run up a slight swale and still have a good chance of a three. I doubted if this hole could be considered ideal, because I feared that, compared with the other Cypress Point holes, there was not a sufficiently easy route for the weaker player. My mind was set at rest a few months ago."

Sixteenth at Cypress Point, circa 1929

36 x 45, oil on panel, 1999 | Course: Cypress Point Club, Pebble Beach, California | Architects: Alister MacKenzie and Robert Hunter

SUNRISE AT RIVIERA'S FOURTH, CIRCA 1995: *Seen here in a dramatic sunrise depiction, Riviera's fourth faces west toward the prevailing winds from off the Pacific Ocean, making its 240 yards seem even longer most days. Miller has presented it after nearly 70 years of play, meaning flying bunker sand has slowly given the bunker a significantly "raised" face. Certainly an example where evolution and heavy play have added to the artistic beauty of the hole and the character of its hazards.*

The real beauty of this hole is that every golfer understands that he can play a safe shot within his capability. But the temptation exists to try a shot one level up from their normal play, if the circumstances seem comfortable or the match is in their favor. Those kinds of balanced options are difficult for an architect to achieve. But when the terrain and the architect work together to create a hole filled with so much temptation, it's the ultimate accomplishment in golf architecture. As Oscar Wilde seemed to be saying of tempting golf architecture, "The only way to get rid of temptation is to yield to it. Resist it, and your soul grows sick with longing for the things it has forbidden to itself."

Sunrise at Riviera's Fourth, circa 1995

36 x 40, oil on panel (1998) | Course: Riviera Country Club, Pacific Palisades, California | Architects: George C. Thomas Jr. and Billy Bell

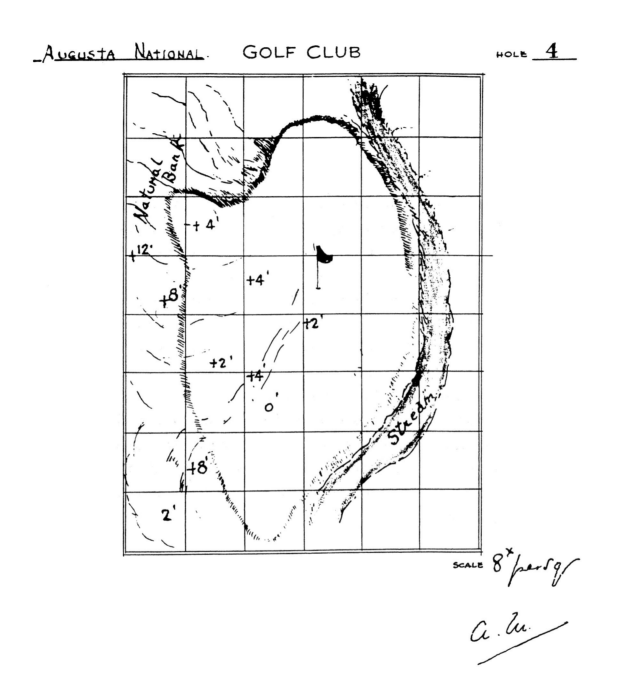

AUGUSTA NATIONAL. GOLF CLUB HOLE 4

Natural Bank

+4'

+12'

+4'

+8'

+2'

+2'

+4

0'

Stream

2'

+8'

2'

SCALE 8ˣ per sqr

a.m.

Alister MacKenzie's Thirteenth Green Complex Rendering

Course: Augusta National Golf Club, Augusta, Georgia | Architects: Alister MacKenzie and Bobby Jones

ALISTER MACKENZIE'S THIRTEENTH GREEN COMPLEX RENDERING: *Besides the creek running the length of this hole, the most tempting element of Augusta's thirteenth is the situation of the green and the contour in its center. Though it has changed for the worse, some of the elements of MacKenzie's and Jones's green design still tempt the player today. The large ridge in the left-center of the green (as sketched here), was designed to tempt players into attacking hole locations near the stream. Knowing the ridge was present allowed players to try to shape shots off the contour to get close to hole locations near the creek edge.*

Note that in the rendering included here, Dr. MacKenzie was still referring to this as the fourth hole. It was the thirteenth in his original routing of the course, but the nines were subsequently switched. After the first Masters the nines were again switched so that this played as the thirteenth hole.

ALISTER MACKENZIE'S THIRTEENTH HOLE RENDERING: *In both the 2000 Masters program and Augusta National's official history, the club stated that this hole "is one that MacKenzie more nearly discovered than designed." I'm sure that this would come as quite a shock to both MacKenzie and Jones, who fretted over this hole and worked to fine-tune its strategy until they were comfortable they had achieved the proper balance between challenge and temptation. Look at this rendering and note the par of "4" listed in the bottom left. This drawing was presented with an article in 1932, the year the course opened. The architects wisely ended up making this a short and tempting par 5, arguably the best hole in golf. The simple change in par injects many factors that a par 4 would not offer, particularly with good players who approach a short par 5 such as this expecting to make birdie. If the hole is listed as a par 4 then they take a different attitude, one that accepts fives more readily because the hole is a difficult par. The difference in competitive play between these two approaches is significant and it's why the par 5s at Augusta National create so much excitement and interest, and also add to the challenge of the holes surrounding them. As Jones said of his philosophy for Augusta National, "We want to make bogies easy if frankly sought, pars readily obtainable by standard good play, and birdies, except on par 5s, dearly bought."*

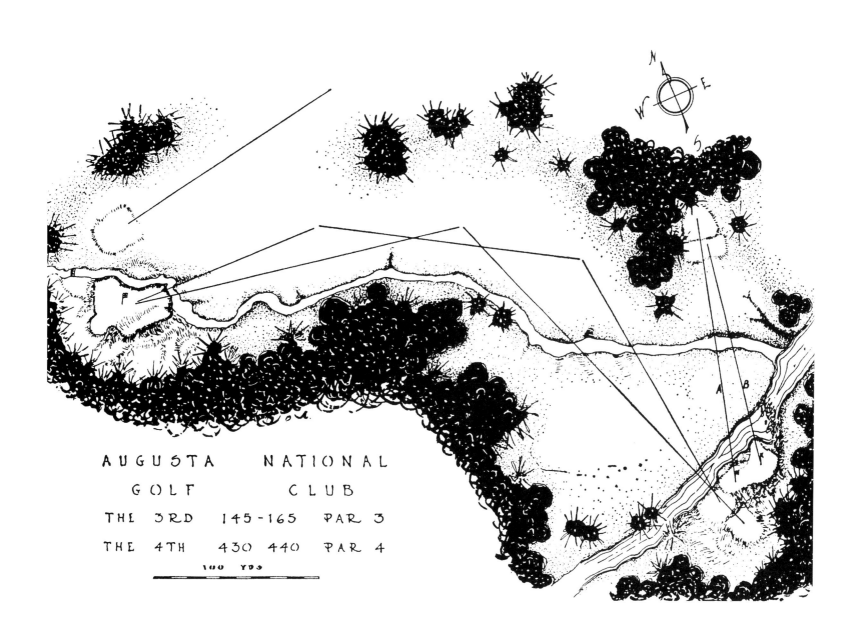

AUGUSTA   NATIONAL

GOLF   CLUB

THE 3RD   145-165   PAR 3

THE 4TH   430 440   PAR 4

100 YDS

Alister MacKenzie's Thirteenth Hole Rendering

Course: Augusta National Golf Club, Augusta, Georgia | Architects: Alister MacKenzie and Bobby Jones

SPRINGTIME AT AUGUSTA NATIONAL'S THIRTEENTH, CIRCA 1933: *One of the most photographed holes in golf, Mike Miller has chosen to present this lovely green setting in its original state, a par 4 of 440 yards that was changed at the outset to 465 yards and a par 5. This is before azaleas popped up along the ridgeline, before more pines had been planted to block out the horizon, and before the greenside bunkers were enlarged and carved out of the rear bank. Thus, the hole may not be recognizable at first glance. But on further inspection we see that Augusta's thirteenth was just as stunning when the two architects "designed" it as it is today. Most of all, its beguiling strategy was in place from day one. The rear bunkers appeared to have been placed in swales that came off the hill, instead of looking like man-made hazards.*

Bobby Jones described the tempting qualities of his hole in his 1960 book, Golf Is My Game*: "In my opinion this thirteenth hole is one of the finest holes for competitive play I have ever seen. The player is first tempted to dare the creek on his tee shot by playing in close to the corner, because if he attains his position he has not only shortened the hole but obtained a more level lie for his second shot. Driving out to the right not only increases the length of the second shot, but encounters an annoying sidehill lie. Whatever position may be reached with the tee shot, the second shot as well entails a momentous decision whether or not to try for the green. With the pin far back on the right, under normal weather conditions, this is a very good eagle hole, because the contours of the green tend to run the second shot close. The chief danger is that the ball will follow the creek. The most difficult pin locations are along the creek in the forward part of the green. A player who dares the creek on either his first or second shot may very easily encounter a six or seven at this hole. Yet the reward of successful, bold play is most enticing. Several tournaments have been obviously won and lost on holes twelve and thirteen. Others, upon careful analysis, will be seen to have been won or lost here, even though the decision may not have been obvious at the time."*

Springtime at Augusta National's Thirteenth, circa 1933

36 x 48, oil on panel, 2000 | Course: Augusta National Golf Club, Augusta, Georgia | Architects: Alister MacKenzie and Bobby Jones

Mid-Ocean's Fifth

36 x 48, oil on panel (2000) | Course: Mid-Ocean Golf Club, Tuckerstown, Bermuda | Architects: C.B. Macdonald and Seth Raynor

MID-OCEAN'S FIFTH: *Known as the "Cape" Hole, the tee shot over Mangrove Lake has become the most widely copied and adapted strategic concept in golf. It's simple, the more you carry, the shorter the approach. The less the player carries, the longer and more difficult the second shot. The Cape is arguably the best of all strategic concepts but is often discouraged in contemporary design because its carry is "unfair" to the shorter hitter. But what interest would there be if every hole were designed to discourage long hitters or eliminate the tempting opportunity to swing away at a drive in hopes of pulling off a heroic shot?*

Architect Charles Blair Macdonald passed along this tale of a site visit at Mid-Ocean in which he was trying to disprove the notion that the carry on the 400-yard par 4 was too long. Macdonald wrote:

"There is a somewhat amusing story connected with the first ball which I ever drove at the Mid-Ocean Club. The Governor General Sir James Wilcox and Admiral Packenham wished to look over the Mid-Ocean development. So they luncheoned with me at the temporary clubhouse. After lunch going over the course we came to the fifth hole, looking over Mangrove Lake. The Admiral doubted if anyone could drive over the water. I explained to him that it was very easy if you did not try to carry too much of the water. He said he would like to see it done; golf balls and clubs were procured and I teed a ball. He asked me where I was going to drive to. There were two dogs about 160 to 170 yards from the tee, one running ahead of the other. I told him I was going to drive where the dogs were. He asked, "Which one" and I said, "The second one," and strange to say, I did and hit the second dog on the rump. I think the Admiral is still telling the story—of what a wonderful golfer I was."

DAYBREAK AT CYPRESS POINT'S SEVENTEENTH, CIRCA 1929: *The seventeenth at Cypress Point, a 420-yard, par 4, maintains Alister MacKenzie's conviction that "water holes should tempt, not torture." Like the sixteenth before it, the carry here can vary depending on the angle the player takes. However, unlike the "Lindbergh thrill" on sixteen, the seventeenth's strategic and tempting qualities are more subtle and probably lost on many players who are anxious to drive their ball to dry land after struggling with the dangerous sixteenth.*

Much has changed since this hole was built. Some of the bunkers depicted in Miller's early morning rendition are gone, most notably those surrounding the clump of cypress trees. Also, some of the fairway to the right of those bunkers has been lost, undermining a bit of the tempting quality created by the architects. But it is modern technology that has undermined the temptation factor on this hole more than on most in golf.

In MacKenzie and Hunter's day, the player could finesse a tee shot along the cliffs, just short of the bunker, with the goal of avoiding a view to the green blocked by the cypress trees. This left a forced carry approach, but a clear view to the green nonetheless. The safe play away from the cliffs results in an awkward approach with trees blocking the view. Subtle contouring around the green along with four well-placed hazards make the approach difficult to land close to the hole. With modern clubs and balls, it is difficult for many players to finesse a shot near the cliff top unless they hit an iron off the tee, which for most players is too great a risk to take. Technology has added one element of temptation for some players: the temptation to drive past the cypress and near the green.

Robert Hunter described the original strategy in 1928: "There is no better hole anywhere than this one which twice crosses the sea. The very long hitter may keep well away from the sea but he must hit 300 yards to open up the hole. The short hitter may take the same route, but he will have three shots to reach home. The medium and very accurate hitter will play close to the sea with his tee shot and play a strong iron or spoon over the sea to the green. A fine group of cypress trees and a nest of bunkers in the center of the fairway at about 270 yards from the tee force the players to choose a definite route to the hole and keep it."

Daybreak at Cypress Point's Seventeenth, circa 1929

31 x 48, oil on panel, originally painted: 2001 | Course: Cypress Point Club, Pebble Beach, California | Architects: Alister MacKenzie and Robert Hunter

The object of golf architecture is to give an intelligent
purpose to the striking of a golf ball.

MAX BEHR

It is important to emphasize the necessity of the golfer
to use his head as much as his hands; or, in other words,
to make his mental agility match his physical ability.

H.N. WETHERED AND TOM SIMPSON

What Is Strategy?

Good old-fashioned golf course design strategy—the element that leads to "tempting" design—is the quintessential component of golf architecture. Tempting strategy is what ultimately separates great holes from merely average ones. The creation of a problem to solve and the presentation of choices, ultimately makes certain golf holes appealing. Without strategy present and decisions to make, courses become uninspiring to revisit.

What exactly defines strategy and how does the architect create it? And what kind of strategic design presents the ultimate in temptation and repeat playing interest?

Heaven knows the concept has been misinterpreted in recent years. Try to ignore what you might have heard for a moment because there is a chance it was inaccurate. (I'm referring to the "if-a-hole-is-physically-difficult-to-par-it-must-be-great" concept, yet another product of tournament golf being allowed to influence design.)

The irony of strategy is that it is such a simple concept.

There is no rational reason why every layout cannot present the player with engaging problems to solve on every hole, without being inordinately penal.

Yet strategy seems to fly over the heads of the select group of people who need to understand it best: those designing and building golf courses today. Too many believe tempting, balanced strategy is created merely by presenting "hard" shots to play. But sound strategy, the kind that makes us want to keep playing some holes over and over, is much more than the mere creation of difficulty. It requires a combination of natural elements incorporated by the architect along with man-made hazards added for the player to deal with.

In a nutshell, strategy is the placement of hazards (bunkers, water, mounds, trees, etc.) in such a way that those hazards make us *think* about how to approach the hole and what our best options for play are. Good strategy gives the player the opportunity to "golf our ball" down different avenues toward the hole. Certain routes are more advantageous than others, with differing degrees of risk involved, depending on the avenue of approach you choose.

Good design strategy shares similarities to a well-designed ski run or obstacle course where a variety of looks and options are presented. And well-conceived strategy incorporates the need to adapt, react, and gauge the value of certain tactics, in similar fashion to the engaging style of uncertainty found in fishing or hunting.

Well-designed strategic holes offer a safe way to navigate the course, but going the safe route may take more strokes to maneuver around trouble. But there are also places where the risk takers or crafty players can make a move to gain some advantage, albeit at great peril.

Strategy is the "intelligent purpose" that sometimes lets short hitters outplay long hitters, and other times will let wise and powerful players be rewarded for putting their talent to shrewd use. On a sound strategic design, certain avenues to the hole are more direct than others. But those more efficient ways offer increased challenge in order to negotiate safely. However, the reward for successfully daring the tougher routes might be a putt for eagle or merely a better angle of approach to a well-bunkered green. Sometimes the strategy is simply a matter of seeing the target better from one side of the fairway versus the other side.

That is golf course design strategy.

Was that so painful?

Evidently there is pain involved in understanding basic design strategy, otherwise how can the lack of its presence be explained in modern design? There are not enough courses being built which ask us to step up to the tee box and think to ourselves, "Let's see now, I should try to play it down the left side in order to have the best angle at that back hole location,

because it looks like today's flagstick is placed behind the bunker on the right corner of the green."

Most of the modern strategy goes more like this: "I need to hit this drive long and straight down the middle because there are bunkers on both sides of the fairway and O.B. on either side of the bunkers. And if I keep my drive on a straight line between those bunkers, I might just be able to hit a four-wood onto that three-tiered green and have a chance at two-putting for par."

Is the difference discernable?

The first example compels a positive, creative, and intelligent plan to approaching the hole, albeit one filled with difficult decisions to make. The second is "penal" in nature and insists on negative thinking. It emphasizes physical play that is dictated by the architect, with no planning required other than to hit the ball long and straight.

The true artist is the golf architect who does not try to tell the player what to do or impose his design on the golfer. The artistic architect presents hazards and options, some more severe than others, but ultimately the designer lets the player decide how to attack based on the course conditions, the match, the weather, and the player's mood.

As Max Behr once said, "On a penal course we see what to avoid. A good shot is the mere evasion of evil. But on a strategic course we must study what to conquer. There are indeed optional safer routes that may be taken...But *the* shot must weather Hell."

Options, risks, mental dilemmas, decisions, mystery solving, intelligence, bravery. That's what strategy is all about. It's why golf prospered from the outset at St. Andrews and continues there today. The Old Course, with its wide fairways, shifting winds, and numerous bunkers placed to require decisions, has more strategic possibilities than any other layout. Architects absorbed those subtle elements early in the century and passed the concept along to their own designs. Key figures like Old Tom Morris, C.B. Macdonald, Alister MacKenzie, Donald Ross, A.W. Tillinghast, George Thomas, Seth Raynor, William Flynn, and many others, took the concept of strategy and even expanded on it in places as any keen artist would. Coincidentally, these great men went on to build virtually all of our most timeless, fascinating American courses. Layouts that some people would give their life savings to play and yet, designs which set standards that modern architecture has not been able to approach in quality.

Where has all the strategy gone? Why are strategic holes apparently so difficult to build?

Numerous elements have influenced the demise of strategy, ranging from the influence of stroke play, to the Great Depression, to the "championship" course setup style, to a simple lack of design education by the architects and their customers. And there have been few, if any, elements working in favor of strategic design that offset the damage done by the abundance of negative influences.

However, it also takes time and effort by the architect to create strategic options that function well. Time in the field before the holes are built, and time during construction to look at a cleared area for play to figure out how best to take advantage of what is available. Time studying the shots of various players is vital as well. And an effort to "market" the architect's "original" ideas is key in this day when golfers consider anything out of the ordinary to be a design defect. Sadly, the first glance is usually the only way courses are evaluated these days, thus architects need to take the time to market their design ideas.

For various reasons—some legitimate, some not—architects rarely take the necessary "in the field" time today. Instead, their energies are focused on the aesthetic appeal of holes, dealing with environmental concerns, or they simply are overburdened by too many projects at one time to devote the necessary effort to fine-tuning individual golf holes. Sure, beauty is vital to making a course desirable to play and enjoy. But ignoring the importance of strategy means losing sight of the real artistic merit of any hole. Those merits lie in the architect's use of the terrain and his ability to incorporate the playing characteristics that will appeal over time.

Interestingly, the widely lauded architects of the early twentieth century predicted that in time, wildly complex and fascinating strategic holes in "the spirit of St. Andrews" would evolve and outdate their own work. They believed the merits of complex strategic holes would soon be understood—holes that everyone could enjoy would win out over dull, difficult, and less enjoyable "penal" designs.

The revolution they spoke of never happened (see What Happened to the Revolution?, page 127).

What we have today are often attractive, well maintained but ultimately shallow golf holes that fail to inspire us after the first or second time around. That's because they have nothing to reveal, no subtle strategic nuances to be discovered. No local knowledge necessary. No mind-boggling obstacles that can be overcome through creative shotmaking. Most holes built today are nice to look at in a magazine photo, but our senses are not interested in mere looks once we get to know them the first time around. As the great philosopher Alistair Cooke writes, "I discovered to my enjoyable relief that a great golf course, like a supreme piece of music, does not reveal its splendors at a first or second reading; nor for most of us, ever."

We must demand substance in our golf holes, just as we expect from any other artistic endeavor designed to add entertainment and joy to our lives. With plenty of golf courses and other hobbies to choose from, we need reasons to keep coming back to certain layouts, just as Alister MacKenzie wrote, "the old stalwarts at St. Andrews do."

That 1920s strategist extraordinaire, Max Behr, was the most vocal figure in warning that the penal style of design was nothing more than a crude, mathematical way to look at golf design.

Whereas the strategic school emphasizes a creative, artistic, and ultimately far more enticing approach, the penal school looks at golf design scientifically, assuming that golf holes should follow formulas with only one logical solution to be drawn.

Well-conceived strategy involves a combination of reason, creativity, temptation, and the unexpected. Strategy is the element most vital to the life of a golf course and the reputation of an architect. That is why, as George Thomas said, the strategy of the golf course is "the soul of the game."

Architectooralooral

BY BERNARD DARWIN, 1927

It seems to me that the great and primary virtue of the modern architect lies in the fact that he did analyze: that he went back to the classic models, and especially to St. Andrews, and insisted on discovering why golfers had for years particularly enjoyed playing particular holes.

Their discoveries came, I think, very briefly to this, that golf at its best is a perpetual adventure, that it consists in investing not in gilt-edged securities but in comparatively speculative stock; that it ought to be a risky business.

Here was something of a new belief founded upon old holes. How those old holes attained the form in which we know them no one can tell. Assuredly it was not owing to the genius of some one heaven-sent designer whose name has unjustly been lost. It was rather through good fortune and a gradual process of evolution.

The holes changed their forms many times according as whins grew or were hacked away, according as the wind silted up sand here or blew it away there, according as the instruments of the game changed so that men could hit farther and essay short cuts and new roads. Yet they possessed some indestructible virtue, so that, however they changed superficially, golfers united in praising them and loved to play them, gaining from the playing of them some pleasing emotion that other holes could not afford. To define that emotion and the cause of it was really to make a discovery, and to proclaim the discovery was to proclaim a new faith.

It was Mr. [John] Low who first put this faith into memorable words, and they are so excellent that I will set them down again here. He is defending the little pot-bunker that is very nearly on the bee-line to the hole and, he says, "The greedy golfer will go too near and be sucked in to his destruction. The straight player will go just as near as he deems safe, just as close as he dare. Just as close as he dare: that's golf, and that's a hazard of immortal importance! For golf at its best should be a contest of risks. The fine player should on his way round the links be just slipping past the bunkers, gaining every yard he can, conquering by the confidence of his own 'far and sure' play. The less skillful player should wreck himself either by attempting risks which are beyond his skill, or by being compelled to lose ground through giving the bunkers a wide berth."

A Triangular Contest

BY H.N. WETHERED AND TOM SIMPSON, 1929

No other game in the world has an architecture of a similar nature of which to boast. A golf course, like a building, must have character and individuality because no one would be content with a mere reproduction. It is the same problem which confronts the architect of a house when he lays out the accessories and is continually adding new features as they suggest themselves. The plan very rarely is completed to accord exactly with the original intention. Walls, roofs, pillars, doors, windows, lawns and gardens are all of them elements capable of alteration in the same way that greens, fairways, hazards and the like admit of rearrangement. The difference is that golf has to do with a form of miniature and open warfare and is on that account subject to an underlying condition of strategy and tactics. The game is something of a triangular contest conducted between one player and another, with the course itself as a third party to be reckoned with as an antagonist, the last of these being the very interesting combatant with whom the architect is primarily concerned. In this sense it is a form of attack and counter attack, because an increased pressure on the part of the player exerts unconsciously a corresponding resistance on the part of designer.

The nature of this silent and mobile conflict depends on the peculiar advantages that golf possesses in regard to its territory. A cricket pitch, a tennis court or a billiard-table are all rigid, cut and dried, symmetrically laid out to be the last inch, capable only of the refinements of workmanship. One may possibly be a shade better than another in point of surface, but that is the most that can be said. You are, in a sense, as regards the majority of games, wearing a shirt cut to the same pattern with a slightly stiffer or softer front. But in golf the kind of shirt you wear admits of a far wider choice; it may be of almost any pattern, material, colour or design.

A golf course, in fact, can be made to adapt itself to almost any conditions. It is not fettered by restrictions beyond those that allow the greatest latitude of play, and it is due to this capacity for unlimited reconstruction that the various tactical opportunities arise.

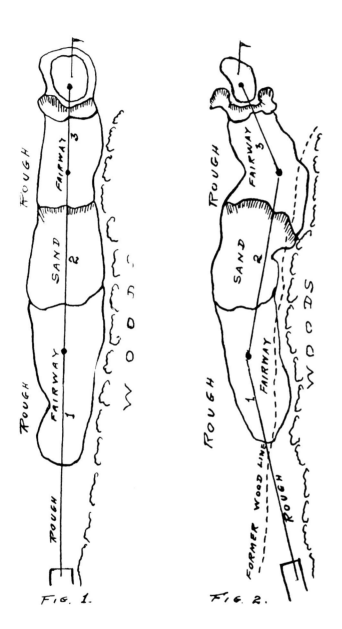

A.W. TILLINGHAST SKETCH OF THE "HELL'S HALF ACRE" PAR 5: *Originally inspired by the seventh at Pine Valley for which A.W. Tillinghast claims to be partly responsible, the concept of the "Hell's Half Acre" hole is sketched and described by Tillinghast: "In my humble opinion the green to the three-shot hole must be beyond the range of any player who misses either his drive or second stroke. Dog-legging enables us to accomplish this. But the most effectual method, and I believe the only satisfactory one, is the location of a truly formidable hazard across the fairway. This must be carried with the second shot if the green is to be gained with the third. Obviously this break in the fairway must be great, let us say 100 yards, for it not only has to be crossed with the second, but also keep any shot short of it from getting home."*

"HELL'S HALF ACRE," PINE VALLEY'S SEVENTH, CIRCA 1927: *Perhaps the most imposing par 5 in all of golf, "Hell's Half Acre", at 578 yards, has been captured by Mike Miller in a rather flattering, almost soothing moment. However, as anyone who has confronted it will tell you, no feeling of calm ever descends over this half acre of Hades.*

Many cite "Hell's Half Acre" as a prime example of "penal school" golf architecture instead of strategic. Sure, the half-acre carry is penal for those failing to clear it. But the decisions involved in whether to layup or carry the hazard are most definitely strategic. George Crump incorporated ideas from many key figures in golf at the time, which helps explain why Pine Valley is the most complete of all designs. Some critics point out that Pine Valley is not genuinely perfect *because it is so difficult for the average player. However, Crump's aim was not to compromise his ideas and appease as many players as he possibly could. His goal was to create a dramatic design with each hole posing a heroic challenge—both mental and physical. He also intended to create something more natural in appearance and character than golf had ever seen, even if it meant a course of greater difficulty. Once an avid hunter (some believe Crump found the site on a hunting expedition), he later banned all hunting on the property. The rule came about because of the love for nature he developed while building the course.*

Chick Evans had this to say about the daring nature of Crump's bold Pine Valley architecture: "Mr. Crump was anxious to see a golf course embodying his ideas of the game and he discovered the possibilities, invisible to many others at that time, of the tree-covered stretch of land, and in the face of many discouragements he went ahead. Nothing was left to chance, and the result is, that to a surprising degree, his ideas have found material form. I remember that when I first played the course I loved it because I thought that it embodied many of my ideals, but I soon discovered that it embodied many more of which I had never thought at all."

"Hell's Half Acre," Pine Valley's Seventh, circa 1927

36 x 48, oil on panel, 2000 | Course: Pine Valley Golf Club, Clementon, New Jersey | Architect: George Crump

Fall Afternoon at Riviera's Ninth, circa 1995

36 x 48, oil on panel, 1999 | Course: Riviera Country Club, Pacific Palisades, California | Architects: George C. Thomas Jr. and Billy Bell

FALL AFTERNOON AT RIVIERA'S NINTH, CIRCA 1995: *Captain Thomas was arguably the boldest design strategist of his time. Not only did he create holes of beauty and originality, he was able to inject touches of subtlety that would give his design work character over time. Riviera's ninth, a 420-yard uphill par 4, embodies everything Thomas aimed to achieve in design. It is lovely to look at, presents a variety of ways to attack the hole, rewards intelligent play, penalizes overaggressive mishits and, finally, gives the average player plenty of room to take a cautious route to the hole. Painted in its "evolved" state, the bunkers have taken on more regularity than Thomas probably would have liked, but they nonetheless remain attractive and imposing.*

Strategically, the hole still mirrors Thomas's shrewd comments from Golf Architecture in America: *"The spirit of golf is to dare a hazard, and by negotiating it reap a reward, while he who fears or declines the issue of the carry, has a longer or harder shot for his second...yet the player who avoids the unwise effort gains advantage over one who tries for more than in him lies, or who fails under the test...the man who knows the value of each of his clubs, and who can work out when it is proper to play one and when to play another, succeeds at the game. The ability of a golfer to know his power and accuracy, and to play for what he can accomplish, is a thing which makes his game as perfect as can be; while a thinker who gauges the true value of his shots, and is able to play them well, nearly always defeats an opponent who neglects to consider and properly discount his shortcomings."*

CYPRESS POINT FIRST HOLE, CIRCA 1929: *Cypress Point's 430-yard first hole is not only beautiful to look at but it also presents subtle strategic possibilities. Though most golfers are just happy to be off the first tee in most any fashion that isn't embarrassing, confident players can start their round aggressively by playing down the right side, over the bunker and the clump of Monterey cypress trees. This not only shortens the hole, but gives the player a flatter lie and a better angle to approach the green. The real beauty of the hole is the area left of the fairway's center, which at one time opened up and connected to the fourteenth fairway. This gave many golfers a false sense of security, allowing them to think they could bail out left, away from the trouble down the right side. However, such a safe shot leaves a very long approach to the green. Today, trees separate the two fairways and narrow the first hole's landing area. Nonetheless, it's still one of golf's most interesting starting holes and, in the days of match competition, made for an especially exciting nineteenth hole.*

Alister MacKenzie summed up the essence of Cypress Point's unique place in the world of golf architecture when he wrote: "There is, first, a natural beauty of surrounding found only on British seaside courses, and added to this is the fascination of wending one's way through woods, over immense sand dunes, to typically inland scenes. It is unsurpassed, having awaited for centuries only to have the architect's molding hand to sculpture a course without peer."

Cypress Point First Hole, circa 1929

36 x 48, oil on panel, 2000 | Course: Cypress Point Club, Pebble Beach, California | Architects: Alister MacKenzie and Robert Hunter

Autumn at The County Club's Fourth Hole

36 x 48, oil on panel (1999) | Course: The Country Club, Brookline, Massachusetts | Architect: William Flynn

AUTUMN AT THE COUNTY CLUB'S FOURTH HOLE: *Portrayed here before the green was rebuilt and subsequently "restored" in a fashion somewhat similar to Flynn's, the fourth at The Country Club's composite course is a classic short par 4 of 340 yards. Not only is it tempting for the fine player who has the chance to drive the green, but the average player has a chance at birdie if he approaches the hole intelligently. The green is blind from the tee, but the player knows a right-to-left shaped shot of some length could utilize the slope leading to the green. It's almost a long Redan par 4 in its styling. The bunkering and the natural beauty of the green complex are typical of Flynn's style. Simple, elegant, and strategically sound.*

Flynn wrote in 1927 on the architect's need to create architecture that pleases all levels of golfer: "An architect should never lose sight of his responsibility as an educational factor in the game. Nothing will tend more surely to develop the right spirit of the game than an insistence upon the high ideals that should inspire sound golf architecture. Every course needs not be a Pine Valley or a National, but every course should be so constructed as to afford incentive and to provide a reward for high-class play; and by high-class play is meant, simply the best of which each individual is himself capable."

LATE SEASON AT BETHPAGE BLACK: *This 455-yard par 4 has only recently been recognized as one of the game's classic strategic two-shotters. Bethpage's Black Course will host the 2002 U.S. Open and has recently been revitalized after years of neglect, though many golfers miss the rustic, weathered look that the bunkers had prior to the project. Built in 1936 by state work crews working for Tillinghast, the Black Course has the least interesting set of Tillinghast greens in the world, which is not detracting much since he was arguably as creative as any designer of greens in the world. Perhaps because the course is so stern and large in scale, Tillinghast decided to keep the greens simple.*

Despite the lack of interest in the greens, the strategy on most of the holes is very sound. The fifth is a standout, featuring a large carry bunker containing small islands of fescue grass. Miller has painted the hole from just in front of this bunker, some 140 yards from the tee. The player who wishes to carry the far end of the sand needs to drive their ball 240 yards. This opens up a view and comfortable angle to the elevated and well-bunkered green. The tendency of most golfers is to play to the left, and to be satisfied with carrying the bunker. However, from the left side, a ridge obstructs the player's view of the green enough that the shot becomes awkward to gauge, even if the player is as close to the hole as the golfer who drove down the right side. It is subtle, simple strategy that ultimately provides the best golf over time.

The fifth at Bethpage provides a fine example of strategy that rewards players with a better glimpse of the hole. Many of the best holes are simply that: offering the player a choice of views of the target. The fifth also demonstrates Tillinghast's theory on design, written in the later years of his life: "When it is more generally realized that a truly fine round of golf represents the accurate fitting together of shots that bear a distinct relation to each other, with the greens opening up to best advantage after placed drives, then the game will be a truer test of all the mighty ones than so many courses now present."

Late Season at Bethpage Black

36 x 48, oil on panel, originally painted: 2001 | Course: Bethpage State Park, Black Course, Bethpage, New York | Architect: A.W. Tillinghast

Bunkers, if they be good bunkers, and bunkers of strong character,
refuse to be disregarded, and insist on asserting themselves; they do
not mind being avoided, but they decline to be ignored.

JOHN LOW

Sunken Pits with Raised Faces

The gracefulness and interest of an architect's green contours speak to us about his artistic touch. As does his cleverness in routing holes that take advantage of natural features, lending subtle touches that only are discovered after many times around a course.

But it's the variety, naturalness, and flair of his bunkers—those sunken pits with raised faces—that differentiate the real artist from the architect who merely lays out golf courses, or worse, those who manufacture landscapes with bunkers bearing a consistently matching "signature."

Legendary golf architect Donald Ross coined the phrase "sunken pits with raised faces" to characterize one of his many styles of bunker design. Yet the phrase captures the essence of a genuinely distinct hazard—a bunker that distinguishes itself as peerless, intimidating, thought-provoking, and sublime.

An outstanding bunker replete with an imposing raised face, rough edges, and a curled-over lip, produces one of the ultimate thrills to overcome in golf. The hazards that stand out as a sign that true artists devoted time and energy to their creation are those bunkers laden with a sense of complete naturalness and dramatic flair. Nothing inspires more adrenaline, fear, and genuine joy than the challenge of dealing with a nasty-looking bunker. The kind that is so rugged-looking it feels like a sandy pit "discovered" by the architect while routing the course and then incorporated into the design.

However, the evolution of the bunker is perhaps the most bizarre change in twentieth century golf. The modern day bunker has been emasculated. Its style and purpose has been transformed from that of an intimidating visual presence to one of so-called "beauty" created by regularly clipped edges or worse, the overgrooming of the sand to make hazards friendlier than the rough.

For the most part, American bunkers tend to be preposterously "clean" and sterile looking. They are too often placed by so-called artists masquerading as architects to "frame" holes or to add "contrast." They are rarely imposing or anything resembling a thought-provoking, artistic-looking hazard. Even at St. Andrews, the irregular faces of the sod wall bunkers have been grassed and cleaned up to look man-made and orderly, a far cry from their roots as old sheep-burrowed holes that evolved into sunken pits with raised faces.

Most frightening of all, apart from the deterioration of the artistic-looking bunker, is the notion that the modern day hazard seldom causes good players to break a sweat. In fact, if the superintendent hasn't packed them down and raked them to play firmer than a fescue fairway, his job is in jeopardy. And, heaven forbid, if the lip of the hazard is not tightly groomed to look like a street curb, the greenkeeper is thought to be letting the course go to seed!

What caused the transmogrification of the bunker from a natural design feature to such an artificial beautification tool for the architect? And worse, how did the bunker become a safe haven for the good player instead of a perilous place that must be avoided? How has the purpose of the sandy hazard gone from an architectural device meant to coerce decision-making and shot placement, to that of a dumb-downed "framing" piece for the modern architect to hold the golfer's hand? After all, in modern day major golf events it is a known fact that the players would rather be in the sand than in the rough. That's right, they'd rather be in the hazard than the nonfairway grass areas. And to top it off, if a hole is not well defined by the bunkers to tell you exactly where to hit it, the architect supposedly has not done his job.

How much more backward can the bunker's role get?

They've gone from serving as hazards to cheap decoration pieces. From posing strategic dilemmas and decisions, to merely sitting around as flashes of sand that tell you how to play and provide you with good lies for recovery play?

There is some hope for the artistic and imposing bunker as we head into the twenty-first century. Many modern architects are trying to reintroduce the notion that bunkers are more than just for framing—that they can be irregularly shaped and natural in appearance while also serving a strategic purpose which adds genuine thrills to a golf hole.

The bunker got its start—where else?—at the Old Course. It is believed that they manifested themselves on that wondrous links when sheep would dig a hole for cold weather protection. Then over time, with help from wind, water, and man, the holes would evolve into sand pits that the golfers would play around.

On the west coast of Scotland, Prestwick's larger expanses of sand offered a different flair. Some even had straight grass-faced or railroad-tie banks. A different style from the pot bunkers of the Old Course, but just as influential in modeling how architects viewed the role of bunkers from a strategic and artistic standpoint. They were hazards. Dangerous, rough, and intimidating.

Alister MacKenzie's irregularly edged, cape and bay bunker style is the most popular of our time and can be traced to the Old Course, namely in the shape of the "Hell" bunker. MacKenzie's style was largely shaped by his mentor, H.S. Colt, who followed Old Tom Morris's lead in absorbing the strategic principles found at St. Andrews, and then expanded on by incorporating the irregular looks of natural dunes. Colt's surreal bunkering at Sunningdale and St. George's Hill was the most stunning early attempt at imitating the lines of nature. They were the first intentionally rugged and dunes-like bunkers that one would assume could only have been created through years of rain, wind, and erosion, but were actually shaped from scratch. And they're still astounding as seen in

Mike Miller's renditions of Sunningdale and St. George's Hill. In more recent times, Pete Dye's bunker style is clearly a tribute to Prestwick and the early American work of C.B. Macdonald, Seth Raynor, and William Langford.

The Old Course and Prestwick merely provided a starting place for architects, because as we know from looking at historic photographs or Miller's landscapes in this chapter, the artistry of bunker building took on new forms as the game evolved and the beauty found in natural dunes was better appreciated.

Architects such as Colt, MacKenzie, Tillinghast, Ross, Macdonald, Thomas, and Flynn instinctively took the basic styles from the proven classics, but like any talented and evolving artist, they added individual touches and new wrinkles as their careers progressed. They expanded on the possibilities while sticking to the proven notion that a natural-looking and natural-playing bunker was the best style of hazard.

The bunker evolved quickly and remarkably during the 1920s, with architects taking more and more chances every time out. They shifted further from any kind of geometric or hard-edged look, and closer to the wind-shaped sand pit style. Almost always, their efforts would push the "naturalness" envelope with the goal of fitting bunkers into the landscapes as artfully as possible. Sure, visionaries such as Macdonald and (occasionally) Tillinghast would go in different directions, by shaping quirky almost-geometric hazards at courses like Chicago Golf Club or Somerset Hills, but even those styles have a certain artistic flair by posing menacing and intimidating bunkers for the player.

Regardless of where the architects derive their inspiration, one underlying principle has always been at the aesthetic soul of classic bunkers: irregularity.

Similar to other features in nature that are shaped by wind and water, the great bunkers have uneven lines and water-eroded edges that seemingly only Mother Nature could create. They mirror the lines and style of nature in their shaping, but also seem charming in the way the architect places them to subtly break up the regularity of a hole.

The words of French impressionist Pierre Auguste Renoir touch on why irregularity is so vital to all art forms. He wrote, "In all the controversies raised daily in matters of art, the capital point to which we are going to draw attention is generally forgotten. We mean irregularity. Nature abhors a vacuum, say the physicists; they could complete their axiom by saying that she abhors regularity no less. If one examines the most famous plastic or architectural productions from this point of view, one quickly perceives that the great artists who created them, careful to work in the fashion of that nature whose respectful pupils they did not cease to be, took good care not to violate her fundamental law of irregularity."

Let's face it: how many golf courses genuinely inspire us when we see two well-groomed cloverleaf "traps" framing the fairway's left side, and another two guarding the right side as if to mirror their counterparts? Over time, is that really natural or attractive to look at? Does that kind of beamed-in-off-the-computer style inspire us to shape a multitude of different shots each time around?

During the zenith of golf design's Golden Age, the artistic possibilities for bunkering reached new heights. Chandler Egan's imitation sand dunes at Pebble Beach, Alister MacKenzie's "floating cloud" bunkers in California, George Thomas and Billy Bell's jagged edged pits at Riviera, and Tillinghast's deep "baseball glove" marvels at Winged Foot were just a few of the more daring artistic efforts to add flare to man-made hazards. And in each case, the artistry was not only a result of care of construction, but also in their ingenious placement. They presented dramatic situations that called on agonizing decisions to be made from the player.

The Great Depression and World War II, however, put an end to these daring efforts and by the time architects began practicing again during the late 1940s, the art form had died. Sterile, cookie-cutter bunkers became the norm as courses were whipped out in assembly-line fashion. Bunkers were expected to be large, perfectly visible, and penalizing, while also embodying a look of cleanliness which obnoxiously announced that man was in control of nature. This resulted in the unnatural-looking oval or cloverleaf style that ruled golf for nearly 30 years. Out were the real hazards, and in was the modern bunker that was supposed to be more practical to maintain and—evidently—even considered attractive.

Today, golf architecture is attempting to come full circle when defining the look and placement of hazards. However, there has been a failure to achieve the kind of results that the Golden Age architects met—in spite of technology that would allow for artistic results with minimal work—because architects and superintendents are caught between a retro movement to restore a certain look, and the mentality of golfers and developers that leans toward the less artistic hazard style of the second half of the twentieth century.

Artistic hazards require time both to build and to evolve. The lack of time devoted to fine-tuning hazard construction or placement has derailed the art of bunker construction. Several contemporary architects construct very attractive hazards, but all too many tend to look awkward because their placement is forced for visibility and "fairness." Instead of picking a great knoll to cut a bunker out of (like the Golden

Age architects consistently did), the modern architect sticks to formulas for the placing of his hazards.

More disturbing is the trend of seeing an architect and his team construct a gem that looks like it's been around for 50 years. But soon after the course opens, some element of the bunker offends those in charge or those playing the course. Perhaps it's the long grass on the bunker lip, or the steep face that can't hold sand and thus exposes the earth below the bunker face (heaven forbid sand should not cover the entire face). This leads to changes in the hazard, and in the future the architect is discouraged from trying to create bold hazards the next time he is given a chance.

Sand Hills in Nebraska is one of the few "accepted" modern courses (i.e., highly ranked) that has presented wildly irregular, ultranatural-looking hazards. And it is in select company because Sand Hills has been praised for the unkempt, "found" look of its bunkers which were carefully crafted by talented men. Few golfers can look at Sand Hills and not be awestruck by the naturalness of the hazards. Yet it is a rare modern example of artistry mixing with well-conceived strategic bunkering. And it will remain that way because Sand Hills has no intention of overmanicuring its hazards to please fairness-minded golf professionals or the local homeowner's association.

Various modern constraints have overtaken the game and yet they have little to do with presenting the everyday player with satisfying, appealing golf. Major tournaments that demand uniform and fair hazards drive the game more than they should. Until the opinions of Tour players are considered secondary factors, the modern architect will always struggle to get artistic bunkers built or to have them maintained as he intended.

Ultimately, the solution to bringing back the artistic bunker lies with the average golfer. The day of the natural and menacing sunken pit with a raised face will not return until there is more understanding from the everyday golfer and a desire to see more intimidating hazards. There must be a tolerance that the ultimate challenge and thrill in golf is a fierce battle with the best nature has to offer, created by an artist with a flair for recreating such art. Anything else just isn't a genuine sunken pit with a raised face.

The Old Course

BY THE ST. ANDREWS LINKS MANAGEMENT COMMITTEE, CIRCA 1985

One would hardly expect to find profound writing in a golf course yardage book. Usually they are oddly conceived road maps to the course you are about to play and rarely is their text so insightful that they amount to anything more than a souvenir remembrance. However, a few years ago the following "Preface to Course Guide" was published in yardage books available for purchase at St. Andrews. The individual author is unknown, but the guide was published by the St. Andrews Links Management Committee. It provides a synopsis of modern day golf design's fear of the past and justifies why the subtle artistry of St. Andrews remains the ultimate in golf architecture:

Modern golf course design philosophy has drifted considerably away from the spirit embodied in the Old Course, which may justly claim to be the archetype for all courses throughout the world. Current practice is influenced by the necessity to build courses on terrain far removed from seaside links, by the corrupting power that earthmoving equipment has bestowed upon golf course designers to move mountains and by a sentiment that the course should be "fair"—which unfortunately often means banality garnished with tricks. The Old Course, in contrast, was modeled by the winds of God that formed the dunes into random and eccentrically complex shapes, indifferent then, as now, to the vanities of men.

The early players obviously exercised a degree of conscious choice as to which part of the links should be greens, but their preference for blind or "sport" shots, may have reflected a greater awareness of the arbitrary nature of fate, in an age when disease and civil strife made life itself more uncertain than it is now. Remember also, when faced with a blind drive or a partially obscure flag-pin, that the course provided recreation for men who might play it a hundred times a year and thousands of times throughout their lives. They would hold a very clear image of what lay behind a screen of gorse or a fold in the ground, so that to them, the judgements of the Fates of the Course were not such a lottery as they appear to a visitor, who may only play a few rounds. It is the uniform judgement of good players that familiarity with the Old Course breeds respect. A wise man does not throw away all his Da Vincis to make way for Picassos or Hockneys, or replace Michaelangelo's David with a work by Moore on the strength of the fashion of a few decades, against which stands the judgement of centuries. We have no intention of reworking our 'Old Master' to suit each transient taste. As a compromise we have produced this course guide which we trust will assist in penetrating some of the obscurities that veil the Old Course, but like the portrait of the Princess will only tell the Knight what she looks like, not the trouble that she will bring him.

What our forebears would have thought of providing a map to play a golf course we would prefer not to contemplate, but tempori parendum. We trust that you will enjoy playing over the Old Course as Robert the Bruce said to his troops before Bannockburn: "I have brought you to the ring, now you must dance."

The Ideal Hazard

BY ROBERT HUNTER, 1926

The construction of hazards on a golf course require[s] much more care and good taste than are usually given it. Next to the greens, the hazards may often be made the most attractive feature in the landscape. Natural hazards are almost always beautiful, and those which are built, whether they be depressions cut in the surface or mounds raised above ground may be made no less so.

All artificial hazards should be made to fit into the ground as if placed there by nature. To accomplish this is a great art. Indeed, when it is really well done, it is— I think it may truly be said—a fine art, worthy of the hand of a gifted sculptor. They should have the appearance of being made with the same carelessness and abandon with which a brook tears down the banks which confine it, or the wind tosses about the sand of the dunes. In nature, rock, tree-roots and turf bind the soil, and when wind or water assails it, the less resistant portions give way, forming depressions or elevations broken into irregular lines. Here the bank overhangs, while there it has crumbled away.

Artificial Hazards—Nature the Model

BY H.S. COLT, 1920

As regards the construction of artificial hollows, mounds, and bunkers, the model should be the natural sand-dune country which is found near the sea. The most noticeable feature about a sand dune is that it has a wide base in relation to its height. It will also be observed that dunes are as a rule to be found in ranges, and do not stand isolated in the middle of a plain. They are usually covered with rough grass or bents. Where the sand is exposed it is always in irregular patches, the shape being dependent on the action of the wind. If sand-dunes be taken as the natural and perfect model, it follows that their characteristics should be reproduced. Sand-bunkers should therefore be cut in irregular shapes, and should be placed in the face of natural hillocks if these exist in the desired positions. If no banks or hillocks are provided by nature they should be constructed artificially, care being taken to give them a base which is broad in comparison with their height, and to make them irregular in outline. Their sky-line should be broken and rolling and hard, straight lines should be avoided. An excellent effect is produced by banking the sand well up on to the face of a bunker cut in a hillock, so that it is visible at a considerable distance.

ST. ANDREWS, SOD WALL BUNKER, CIRCA 1925: *One of St. Andrews' famed sod-wall bunkers is painted by Mike Miller as it would have looked in the 1920s. Note the irregular, rustic appearance of the bunker face. The bunkers at St. Andrews define the ultimate in temptation because there are 121 of them and each seems to come into play at some point during a round for every golfer. Yet each offers the tantalizing option to play left, right, short, or over them. They tantalize and provoke thought like no other bunkers in the world. Some of their allure has to do with their placement. Much has to do with their small size in relation to the rather wide style of the course.*

Robert Hunter was among many early writers to sum up the Old Course's merits and to clarify the beauty of this ultimate strategic course:

"It is rather difficult to explain why St. Andrews should be the one and only course which stands above and scorns all criticism. One can say evil things of Sandwich, Prestwick, Hoylake, or any other course, and find some to agree; but if one assails the home of the Royal and Ancient, one soon finds that the atmosphere grows chilly. I suppose the reason for this lies in the fact that no one can play the Old Course for a few weeks without finding himself a victim to its subtle and overpowering fascination. Power, always so impressive in golf, is there often so futile when pitted against skill and cunning. The strategy required to play some of the holes is so varied and so interesting. Moreover, a few of the holes are never to be forgotten. Pine Valley is a course where we hit with all our power, and if the high-soaring ball plumps down on a bit of turf, we are immensely pleased; but we never have a sufficient variety of shots or quite enough skill and accuracy to play St. Andrews as we should like to play it. At Pine Valley we feel that we lack power only, and no one thinks of committing suicide because Dempsey can lick him; but at St. Andrews our brains fail us. There is something in the very terrain which outwits us. That is, I think, what gives the Old Course its enduring vitality. It is the most captivating and unfair, the most tantalizing and bewitching, of all courses."

St. Andrews, Sod Wall Bunker, circa 1925

27 x 24, oil on panel, 2000 | Course: The Old Course, St. Andrews, Scotland | Architects: Mother Nature with help from Old Tom Morris and others

Dunes at Tenby, Wales, circa 1990

24 x 21, oil on panel, 1997 | Course: Tenby Golf Club, Dyfed, Wales | Architect: C.K. Cotton

DUNES AT TENBY, WALES, CIRCA 1990: *Depicted here are dunes along the fourth hole at C.K. Cotton's Tenby Golf Club. Cotton practiced golf course design after World War II and wisely left these dramatic dunes alone at Tenby.*

Luther Burbank's words remind one of how vital it is for any builder, particularly golf architects, to respect nature and preserve its best features: "Nature's laws affirm instead of prohibit. If you violate her laws, you are your own prosecutor, judge, jury and hangman."

RUSTIC BUNKERING ON SUNNINGDALE'S FIFTH, CIRCA 1925: *Constructed in 1922, Colt's bunkering on the New Course was unlike anything seen in golf then—or now. Redefining "natural," this medium length par 3 of 162 yards features some of the most artistic hazard work ever created. It's difficult, as Robert Hunter once said, to tell where art ends and nature begins. Mike Miller has portrayed the hazards in their most dramatic, rustic style. His colors here prove that a golf hole can be attractive to look at even with so few shades of green.*

Rustic Bunkering on Sunningdale's Fifth, circa 1925

29 x 40, oil on panel, 1998 | Course: Sunningdale Golf Club, New Course, Berkshire, England | Architect: H.S. Colt

Eighth at St. George's Hill, circa 1925

36 x 48, oil on panel, 2000 | Course: St. George's Hill Golf Club, Surrey, England | Architect: H.S. Colt

EIGHTH AT ST. GEORGE'S HILL, CIRCA 1925: *Built in 1913, Colt's 175-yard par-3 eighth features one of the most impressive green complexes in all of golf architecture. The deep bunkers cut out of the base of a ridge are set well short of the tiny green, and yet the whole complex intimidates when viewed from an elevated tee. Note how small the green is in relation to the overall green complex, and how the tightly mown fairway grass atop the ridge will no doubt leave many fascinating short game shots for those missing the green.*

Colt and Alison wrote of bunkers: "The normal object with which the remainder of bunkers are placed is to introduce an element of risk into the game. The player is tempted to try either to carry or to skirt a bunker. He is offered a reward for success and a penalty for failure. It is evident, however, that the reward and the penalty should bear a due proportion to one another. If the penalty is unduly severe, few players will feel tempted to take the risk; while if the penalty is almost negligible, no daring will be required and no thrill will be experienced."

ROYAL COUNTY DOWN BUNKER STUDY: *This deep sand pit at Royal County Down is one of many attractive bunkers to be found on this magnificent course. This fairway bunker sits on the left side of the second hole. A ball finding it results in a difficult recovery, made more intimidating by the top edge's overhanging fescue grasses.*

In the modern day interpretation of the hazard, many would consider this bunker unfair because balls could be lost in the attractive fescues. They could also roll up underneath the "lip" and cause a golfer to incur a penalty for an unplayable ball. The PGA Tour would order this fescue chopped back for tournament play because it could cause an "unfair" moment to occur. But is that really the direction and style our hazards should take? To act as elements of design that show up for appearances' sake, but bear no genuine intimidation or penalizing factor? Consider Robert Hunter's words before you suggest we must strive to make our hazards "fair" and less of an intimidating factor in golf:

"There can be no real golf without hazards, and unless these be varied, plentiful, and adroitly placed there will be no great golfers. Hazards are the decisive influence in the making of golfers. They fashion the shots of the youth. Let the greens be well guarded and the youth will soon learn to pitch and stop. With undulations before him, he will become adept at placing his shots—whether pitching or running. Build pits on the borders of the fairways and he will learn to keep down the middle, and give him a few heroic carries to make and the results will be all that can be desired."

Royal County Down Bunker Study

18 x 20, oil on panel, 1997 | Course: Royal County Down, Newcastle, Northern Ireland | Architects: Old Tom Morris; revisions by Seymour Dunn, Harry Vardon

Breezy Day at Baltimore Country Club, before Opening, circa 1926

12 x 24, oil on panel, 1997 | Course: Baltimore County Club East Course, Baltimore, Maryland | Architect: A.W. Tillinghast

BREEZY DAY AT BALTIMORE COUNTRY CLUB, BEFORE OPENING, CIRCA 1926: *Some of the ultimate "sunken pits with raised faces" can be found at Baltimore County Club's Tillinghast layout. Depicted here by Mike Miller shortly before the course opened for play, the bunker faces are covered in nasty rough that is offset by the short fairway cut. The contrast makes the bunkers look even more imposing than they actually are. In fact, this is a relatively easy wedge shot even though it is played off a slight downhill lie. But the tier in the green, combined with the deep bunkering, makes the short par-4 seventh of 344 yards seem much more difficult than it really is.*

The visual and mental intimidation elements of a hazard play a key role in how they affect play. In today's style of manicuring hazards to appear kinder and gentler, hazards have lost much of their dramatic flair. Moreover, when difficult rough surrounds fairways and greens, well-manicured hazards becomes even less significant, to the point we hear some players preferring they end up in sand instead of the nearby rough.

Tillinghast wrote of the role of hazards in 1914:

"Hazards are frequently natural—a brook, a pond, a swamp, a road or an abandoned excavation, etc., but for the most part they have been placed by the golf architect. These artificial hazards are usually sand pits so located as to trap badly-hit balls. They are the inanimate fielders of golf, and all golfers strive to follow Keeler's precept of 'hitting 'em where the fielders ain't.' In brief, the hazards of golf put a premium on the accurate placement of the ball. The mediocre player fears them and cramps his strokes in the effort to avoid them, and his play will not improve until he learns to go at a hazard fearlessly."

SUNRISE AT CYPRESS POINT, SECOND HOLE, CIRCA 1998: *Originally, the tee shot at Cypress Point's second hole was required to carry an area of dunes. Over a period of 70 years though, that area became manicured and eventually was turned into three distinct bunkers. Problems with occasional washouts probably also played a major role in turning this dunes area into defined bunkers.*

Certainly regular and manicured in style, these bunkers have been captured by Mike Miller in an early morning light that reveals their character, depth, and beauty. Though these three bunkers do not fit MacKenzie's irregular style of hazard construction, they nonetheless are attractive and present a problem from the tee. Whether purists like it or not, certain kinds of hazard evolution must be accepted—either because of heavy play, improved aesthetics, maintenance needs, or because the change is simply unavoidable. At St. Andrews, many bunkers showed up over time thanks in part to sheep burrowing holes and wind shaping new sunken pits. Robert Hunter also shared this thought on the evolution of the bunkers at St. Andrews, which reminds us that courses are ever changing. Sometimes such natural additions can add to the strategy and artistic beauty of courses:

"I am told, although it seems a bit incredible, that where divots are not carefully replaced and many such wounded spots are long neglected, a big wind may at times carve out a bunker. It is a tradition that this is what happened at St. Andrews, and that it explains why many of the sand traps are on the direct line to the hole. Whether or not this be true is not as important as the fact that they are now there...Golf there could hardly have been as interesting before these hazards existed as it is today."

Sunrise at Cypress Point, Second Hole, circa 1998

24 x 36, oil on panel, 1999 | Course: Cypress Point Club, Pebble Beach, California | Architects: Alister MacKenzie and Robert Hunter

After the Rain at Merion

24 x 35, oil on panel, 1997 | Course: Merion Golf Club, East Course, Ardmore, Pennsylvania | Architects: Hugh Wilson and William Flynn

AFTER THE RAIN AT MERION: *The crafty thirteenth at Merion is one of golf's most beloved short par 3s at 127 yards. It's also one of the most artfully bunkered, with the large guarding hazard making the shot into this green both intimidating and exciting. Over the years, flying sand has built the front lip so high that balls in the front third of the green can't be seen. Many modern day players don't like having to wait until their 130-yard walk to the green to find out where they have landed, but that kind of "in-between" anticipation of knowing the outcome of a shot was often referred to by the master architects as adding to the game. They believed it was another subtle thrill to make the walk from tee to green that much more fun. This was one reason many of the older architects did not shy away from blind holes that provide the ultimate anticipation of knowing your end results. Merion's thirteenth provides a lesser version of such a thrill.*

Note the grasses planted in the bunker. William Flynn assisted Hugh Wilson on the original construction of Merion's East Course, and was responsible for its remodeling in 1924. In many of his later courses, Flynn built large bunkers with fewer "capes and bays" than his fellow Philadelphians George Thomas and A.W. Tillinghast. However, Flynn did break up the areas of sand by planting grasses that both added to the aesthetics and also injected unpredictability to his hazards. The thirteenth is cut out of a gentle up-slope, which Flynn wrote was the best way to build attractive hazards: "A concealed bunker has no place on a golf course because when it is concealed it does not register on the player's mind as he is about to play the shot and thus loses its value. The best looking bunkers are those that are gouged out of faces or slopes, particularly when the slope faces the player. They are very much more effective in that they stand out like sentinels beckoning the player to come on or keep to the right or left."

The Art of Golf Design

BUNKER STUDY, THIRTEENTH AT TALLGRASS: *Recognizing William Flynn's use of fescue and other grasses in the bottom of bunkers, Gil Hanse is one of many architects returning "islands" to modern day bunkers. Golden Age architects such as MacKenzie, Maxwell, Thomas, and Flynn frequently used grassy islands to lend a little zest and drama for players who hit wayward shots into larger expanses of sand. After all, bunkers are supposed to provoke some fear of the unpredictability of landing in a hazard. What better way to make a player steer a shot away from a hazard by letting them know that a misplay could result in any number of awkward stances or lies caused by grassy islands?*

Any disruption of normal sandy areas in bunkers disappeared over the years as superintendents understandably found islands and other native grasses too difficult to maintain. This is a sensitive issue with architects because they view their work like any other art, and expect their vision to be maintained in some fashion.

Could we ever forgive a museum director for simply putting a classic painting in storage because it is too difficult to light or its frame is hard to clean? Art requires careful maintenance like anything else, and in golf architecture we find the hardest balance of all because of normal wear-and-tear, aging, and natural elements changing an architect's vision. The good news is, modern maintenance practices have become so refined that a talented superintendent can find creative ways to maintain "islands" without it taking away too much time from their primary maintenance. And besides, as we see in the Tallgrass study here, the less maintenance for bunkers, the more we find interest, drama, surprise, and natural beauty.

Bunker Study, Thirteenth at Tallgrass

20 x 24, oil on panel, 2000 | Course: Tallgrass Golf Club, Shoreham, New York | Architect: Gil Hanse

I do not remember having met any golfer who did not consider himself on the whole a remarkably unlucky one...However unlucky you may be, it really is not fair to expect your adversary's grief for your undeserved misfortunes to be as poignant as your own.

HORACE HUTCHINSON

Luck and Wind

After the late 1970s publication of Michael Murphy's *Golf in the Kingdom*, there has been an ongoing campaign by the book's followers to remind us that golf, more than anything else, is "a metaphor for life."

I'm here to tell you that I concur. Golf is, in fact, a metaphor for life.

So can we all agree and get back to talking about the elements of the game that genuinely contribute to its widespread appeal? Do we really take up the game and pursue it with passion because of its metaphoric offerings?

Personally, I'd like to think that the most enduring elements of golf would include the extensive variety of courses, the natural setting the sport is played in, and the intriguing characters who play the game. These elements should take priority over golf's intriguing but not particularly satisfying metaphoric offerings.

Can't we, like trial lawyers, just stipulate this fact to the jury and move on?

On second thought, no.

Let's run with the golf-is-a-metaphor-for-life obsession for a moment to discuss an element of golf whose symbolic offerings are disregarded to the detriment of the game and the art of course design.

It is an undeniable fact that luck plays a substantial role in both life and golf. Yet many golfers—many of the same ones who curl up to a fireplace and read the latest metaphysical metaphoric romp through golf—will also be the first of our golfing brethren to advocate that golf architects and superintendents must do everything in their power to eliminate luck from intervening in their weekly game.

"Smooth out those greens!" they'll cry.

Or, "Rake those bunkers twice a day so my ball won't get buried."

"Plant trees in straight rows so that those wild hitters are punished and there is no opportunity for those dashing, courageous, skillful recovery shots."

Or my favorite from touring professionals: "It rained a tenth of an inch last night, so we must play lift-clean-and-place today in order to ensure equity for the entire field!"

These complaints about unfairness or other unfortunate breaks have been a part of golf from the beginning, but never has the game yielded to the notion of fairness like it does in its current version.

With the element of chance lurking, we feel a certain "never over until it's over" sense to our matches. And because we know that there is always the chance that serendipity could intervene to save us (or spell disaster), we never give up hope on the golf course. Nor does the wise player ever get complacent.

Even with the knowledge of what a fascinating element luck provides, the modern architect—mostly at the direction of the golfing masses—seemingly goes out of his way to eliminate randomness and emphasizes predictability.

Let me explain.

Our courses, first and foremost, should be designed to promote skillful and thoughtful play. Hazards and greens should be created that bring out our best and inspire us to pull off shots we never could have imagined. They should be designed in such a way as to ask us to take risks that will open up wonderful possibilities. They should ask us to shape shots and create imaginative solutions to problems that are presented, often forcing us to decide between easier and more difficult options. The various hole locations, bunkers, tee positions, and other elements should require that golfers think their way to the hole and use whatever avenue seems best to get there in the fewest strokes possible.

Yet, in modern design's so-called effort to promote genuine skill and inspire our senses, golf architecture has lost sight of its purpose. The architect seemingly goes out of his way to eliminate the lucky shot or the unexpected and to reward only the long, high, straight shot. Proven strategic design concepts are forgotten in that effort to ensure what is perceived as fair and just. Hazards are only fair if placed on the sides of the fairways, meaning that the only avenue to the hole is on a long, straight line from tee to green.

Meanwhile, the inspirational, tempting, and strategic philosophy puts the hazards in places that require intriguing decisions, with penalties awaiting for poor choices, mishit shots or—dare I mention?—the occasional bad bounce.

On the maintenance side of golf, where the obsession with eliminating luck has reached new lows, hazards are created to permanently swallow up balls (such as tall grasses in ditches), or hazards are only fair if they prop balls up so well that luck is eliminated from rearing its head (see bunkers that give the players better lies than the fairways do). For some unknown reason, golfers demand this extreme "either-or" situation instead of understanding the exciting nature of a more arbitrary, unpredictable situation, one that can even lead to the most satisfying of all shots: the heroic recovery.

This desire for predictability and the elimination of luck strips charm from the sport. That's because there is often a genuine thrill in finding a ball and then trying to extricate oneself from trouble. There is a certain excitement and passion that you can develop from playing golf when hazards allow you to hold out hope of finding your ball and, just possibly, getting to play it.

Robert Hunter once wrote, "Great golfers would find the game stupid if no occasion arose to use the more difficult shots in their repertoire. The keenest delight in golf is given to those who, finding themselves in trouble, refuse to be depressed, and, with some recovery, snatch from their opponents what seemed for them certain victory."

There have always been those who want to do everything humanly possible to strip a course of its potentially unlucky elements. In recent years we've seen architects and developers willing to spend thousands—even millions—of dollars to shift gobs of soil so that any kind of undulation potentially blocking perfect visibility to the hole is eliminated, and thus everyone has a "fair" chance to see the target. Fairways are "bowled" at great expense to funnel balls back to the middle, all to supposedly make the game less punishing and fun. Courses are routed on properties so that a majority of the holes play downhill, promoting the all-important "visibility." Architects are instructed to, or willingly provide, a blatant road map to their holes, which certainly is helpful the first time around, but on return visits gives the golfer nothing to figure out, and thus, renders all too many holes boring.

The worst result of all this antifate, antirandom, antiluck design and construction is the loss of any strategic value to the course or any genuine opportunity to reward fine play. The luck-ridding mentality leads to contrived designs and golfing battlegrounds that fail to induce thinking or inspired play. And when there is little inspiration, the art dies.

In the modern way of thinking, bunkers are used to close up openings to greens so that run-up approaches can't be used during a daring recovery from the woods, or worse, their impetus is to merely stop the underhit shot. Bunkers are often placed for negative or penal reasons, not with captivating and strategic intentions.

And the maintenance expectations for hazards is where hypocrisy genuinely rears its ugly head. The bunkers, meant to penalize shots, are then expected to have perfectly firm bottoms raked immaculately each day because anything else would be "unfair." If the bunker conditions are not perfect or a recovery directly at the hole is not possible, golfers cry that the superintendent is not doing his or her job.

Another expected effect of the antiserendipity mode of modern day golf is the tenet that all putting greens must be tilted from back to front (toward the approaching golfer). This is so that all shots hitting the surface, even those struck in mediocre fashion, are "held" by the green. And when, heaven forbid, all 18 greens on the course are not of consistent firmness and speed, once again the superintendent is labeled a failure for not providing "fair" playing conditions.

You cannot eliminate lucky elements from finding their way into golf without the consequence of taking adventure and joy out of playing a hole. This is a sport that offers a leisurely, sometimes exciting battle with nature's offerings (or at least, that is how it gained its initial popularity). Yet, many in the sport seem to have lost focus on the big picture, viewing golf as a life or death matter where a stroke of bad luck in the form of a bad lie, a blind shot, or a firm green is the ultimate evil. And those in power who don't do everything in their power to eliminate luck are harming the sport.

There is still a core of wise golfers who pick up on the elements of a course and store the information in their brains. Many figure out which greens are softer than others, or which bunkers tend to produce nasty lies. That is called local knowledge. It's using your brain to outsmart the course or your opponent, and it's the easiest way to eliminate luck.

H.N. Wethered and Tom Simpson wrote a witty, brilliant book titled *The Architectural Side of Golf* (1929). In it they talk about almost everything relating to golf course design, life, and poetry. Yes, poetry. Among their concerns for the future of course design was the element of the game that people were threatening to change even back in 1929. The elimination of luck and the inability of many golfers to accept that a certain kind of unpredictable fate was part of the game:

...it must be kept in mind that the elusive charm of the game suffers as soon as any successful method of standardization is allowed to creep in. A golf course should never pretend to be, nor is it intended to be, an infallible tribunal. Certain degrees of luck, it is true, can reasonably be judged criminal - as, to take one example, when a fold in the ground is so sharp and boldly pronounced that a matter of inches will determine a very wide deflection in the direction a ball will take to the one side or the other. At St. Andrews the slopes are never abrupt to this degree, but invariably so shallow that frequently either side of a slope can be made use of in order to get near the pin.

The object of the profuse introduction of bunkers and large spaces of green is, it is frankly admitted, to eliminate chance to the utmost possible extent. Competitive golf is chiefly responsible for this tendency to design courses on principles of absolute and relentless justice. The insistent theme, where great stakes are at issue, is that the good shot (by which is meant the shot that is perfectly struck) should receive its exact equivalent. Two flawless strokes, such is the argument, where the hole demands them, and an immaculate putt, should on every possible occasion register a three. In the old spirit of golf, however, two and two frequently made five. The "luck" was regarded as part of the legitimate fun of the game, without which as a sport the game would suffer. The attraction that counted the most was the test of ingenuity in getting round difficulties and overcoming new and unexpected situations. In the final result the best man generally won. If he did not, it merely went to prove that there is no infallible system possible even to the most modern of us.

Another victim of the antiluck obsession has been the view of wind and its influence on the courses we build and play. Gusty breezes and steady blasts are viewed as promoting luck, and more courses than ever are built in places protected by wind to escape those dreaded, unpredictable gusts of air. But few things in the game are more fascinating than a well-designed hole with the added, unpredictable element of wind.

The combination of the two provides the ultimate in variety, as well as inviting decision-making, temptation, and reward for great skill. Early pioneers in golf like C.B. Macdonald believed that wind was perhaps the most essential element in the game if the architect was attempting to present a varied and constantly interesting design. They felt that it separated precision play from less accurate play and that on a day with any wind and on a course of even remotely creative design, the best players would be rewarded for careful planning and creative execution of shots. Today, soft turf, trees, and an aerial target style of golf have become the dominant and revered natural features in American golf. Anything else is seemingly considered odd, if not downright freakish.

In this modern-day desire to "control" the game at all costs, the negative view of wind was forever changed by the migration to inland sites. Though they may be beautiful, they certainly present a less varied and interesting canvas for golf. Once considered an essential element to the day-to-day interest and variety of design, wind is now seen as an unfair and unpredictable fluke that interferes with great golf architecture.

The present view of wind was publicly articulated in 1998 when professional golfer David Duval, a well-read gentleman who normally chooses his words prudently, stated during the British Open that wind introduces too many elements of luck to golf. He implied it was preferable to hold major events where there is less wind.

Duval later shifted his position when he realized that as one of the most intelligent and physically talented players in the world at the time, he was at a distinct advantage in those supposedly flukish elements. The harder the wind blows, the more his shrewd thinking and ability to hit solid shots is rewarded. In wind, his talent is separated from those less able to handle the conditions.

As turf conditions have become incredibly refined and PGA Tour professionals grow more spoiled by remarkable maintenance or designs that present few if any quirks, they have forgotten that golf is as much a battle of chance as any-thing else. It is a test of mental strength against nature's most offbeat and challenging offerings. Yet, many golfers have absorbed the mentality that architecture and the elements should not get in the way of a lovely walk in the park.

A green sloped away from the fairway, a gust of wind, an unlucky bounce, and hazards placed in thought-provoking places are now seen as poor design elements that must be avoided.

They supposedly spoil the walk, not add to its charm.

How did golf, whose foundation was built on nature's randomness and constant unpredictability, drift so far from its roots?

Natural Golf and Legislation

BY MAX BEHR, 1922

If golf is always to give of its best there is required upon the part of our authorities a perfect sensing of the equilibrium that must be maintained between the two factors that go to make it: the player with his instrument, and nature. Before the advent of inland golf, and later the small heavy rubber-wound ball, this equilibrium was never a consideration; golf was played upon the turf of links land which had never known a lawn mower, and as the golfer accepted the lie of his ball, never questioning whether the grass long or short, in the same way he accepted the natural hazards with which such land abounded. Then the feather ball first, and later the gutta, never allowed him to look upon the wind with impunity, and consequently when the elements were not propitious he was driven to consider intimately the configuration of the ground and its effect upon his endeavors to cheat the wind with a low-played shot.

Common sense dictated the choice of situations for the hole; it was only natural that such situations should be achievable, but he was also governed in his choice by a fine stretch of turf regardless of the wind holes that had exposed the substrata of sand. And, after all, why should he worry about an ominous looking pit that had eaten its way into the place he wished to dig the hole? It was as fair to one as it was to the other; and as the ancient golfer was never obsessed with his score, what if such a pit meant the death of his hopes? Golf was only the more exciting.

Golf was then in that fortunate state when it never entered the mind of the golfer that he could vie with nature. The building of inland courses was unthought of, and consequently his mind was undisturbed with the inevitable evolving of principles to govern such an artificial undertaking. He went out to battle with an opponent with no idea in his mind that fortune should bestow its favors equally. If his ball got into more rabbit scrapes or cuppy lies than did his opponent's, he might rail against his bad luck, but he never questioned that it was as much a part of the game as anything else. And he knew that he had with his wooden clubs and feather or gutta ball instruments, which, used with skill, were equal to the tasks he had to accomplish, but he was unsophisticated to any idea that he could overwhelm nature, and hence was deserving of certain rights which the present small heavy ball and the delicately perfected iron clubs of today have bred in the mind of the modern golfer.

What is the cry we hear today—this or that is unfair! A golfer comes in from a round, and some bunker or green has spoiled his score, and he proceeds to damn the course and the whole world. And all this because he approaches golf selfishly, with such an exaggeration of ego that he is convinced he is not only equal to coping with nature, but that he should never be humbled by her.

Now this modern attitude of mind is most regrettable. It has been caused by three things: the transplanting of golf inland with a consequent development of principles governing what a course should be; the entrance of minds tutored upon games and hence expecting a fair reward of skill, and the development of clubs and balls to a point which has given the golfer the effrontery to say what must be.

Instead of the golf architect taking links land as the example to copy, he is now forced to consider the idiosyncrasies of the modern ball. Instead of nature dominating golf, it is now dominated by the mechanical devices of man. This is the unhealthy state to which golf has arrived, and the psychological tendency is to make further inroads upon nature's side of the balance, for once the human mind succeeds in overcoming natural hazards in life it never remains satisfied until it has devised means to do away with them altogether.

I do not mean to imply that it is possible to return to those halcyon days of golf, or that it is even desirable; but what I do wish to emphasize is that unless we keep before us a true perspective of golf, a viewing of it always from its natural side, it will eventually degenerate to a known quantity, a true game, and will become robbed of those elements of mystery and uncertainty which make every round a voyage of discovery.

The fate of golf would seem to lie in the hands of the Royal and Ancient Golf Club and the United States Golf Association. Can we expect that they will protect and reverence the spirit of golf?

LATE AFTERNOON ON SAND HILLS' EIGHTEENTH: *Opened in 1995, Sand Hills has emerged as the most significant design effort of the last half of the twentieth century. Much of its strength lies in its inventive design and the return of certain architectural characteristics rarely found in contemporary design. Most notably, Sand Hills requires ground shots, imaginative short game play, and the acceptance that luck will both help and hurt you during a round here. The bunkers are not raked and the native grasses can be punishing. Meaning: the golfer will find misfortune, but usually because of his own mistakes.*

Few courses today create such an unpredictable environment for golf and yet still receive accolades. Equity is the top requirement all too often and the need for "fair" golf consistently impacts an architect's ability to present dramatic architecture. But Sand Hills presents many holes such as the long par-4 eighteenth, a 467-yarder, where skill is required, sound play rewarded, and stunning natural hazards must be overcome. Coore and Crenshaw are great admirers of C.B. Macdonald, who in 1927 insisted on the need to prevent "equity" from overtaking golf architecture:

"So many people preach equity in golf. Nothing is so foreign to the truth. Does any human being receive what he conceives as equity in his life? He has got to take the bitter with the sweet, and as he forges through all the intricacies and inequalities which life presents, he proves his mettle. In golf the cardinal rules are arbitrary and not founded on eternal justice. Equity has nothing to do with the game itself. If founded on eternal justice the game would be deadly dull to watch or play. The essence of the game is inequality, as it is in humanity. The conditions which are meted out to the players, such as inequality of the ground, cannot be governed by a green committee with the flying divots of the players or their footprints in the bunkers. Take your medicine where you find it and don't cry. Remember that the other fellow has got to meet exactly the same inequalities."

Late Afternoon on Sand Hills' Eighteenth

32 x 38, oil on panel, 1997 | Course: Sand Hills Golf Club, Mullen, Nebraska | Architects: Bill Coore and Ben Crenshaw

Sunrise at Pebble Beach's Seventeenth, circa 1929

24 x 36, oil on panel, 1998 | Course: Pebble Beach Golf Links, Pebble Beach, California | Architects: H. Chandler Egan (routing by Jack Neville and Douglas Grant)

SUNRISE AT PEBBLE BEACH'S SEVENTEENTH, CIRCA 1929: *No "experiment" was ever so bold in the annals of golf architecture as Chandler Egan's redesign of Pebble Beach in 1929. He took a geometric and often clumsy design that was set within an ingenious routing, and crafted natural looking dunes. These "imitation sand dunes" on the 218-yard, par 3 not only presented thrilling shots but were also placed in a strategic manner that dictated shrewd play. The "dunes" received a positive reception when they debuted during the 1929 U.S. Amateur at Pebble Beach, but they slowly disappeared soon after when the resort fell on hard times and maintenance budgets were minimal.*

If attempted today, the imitation dunes would be shot down in the name of fairness. Their unraked, potentially scorecard-wrecking nature would not be allowed with today's emphasis on stroke play taking priority above all else. Though we all enjoy hazards that allow us to recover, certain thrills are missing from golf by not having to overcome such perilous and dramatic hazards.

Egan contemporaries H.N. Wethered and Tom Simpson wrote extensively on the issue of luck and stroke play in The Architectural Side of Golf. *This is among many fine passages on the subject:*

"What is 'fair' for the one is regarded as the grossest injustice by the other. It falls to the lot, therefore, of the architect—in this case not always the happiest—to weigh the claims made on him as an impartial arbiter and to decide the issue according to the best of his judgement. He will not allow, if he can help it, the unduly powerful to terrorize the rest of the field with impunity, nor will he permit the weakest to go to the wall without a protest. In this laudable endeavor he is actuated by the best and most disinterested motives. His object is to encourage enthusiasm, mental agility and happiness in the hearts of all good golfers whether they be merely magnificent, passably good or totally indifferent. At the same time he must punish willful extravagance and ensure that the virtuous are rewarded."

WINDY DAY AT DORNOCH, WHINNY BRAE HOLE: *One of the simplest but most intimidating short par 3s in golf is the 165-yard sixth at Royal Dornoch. Playing to a perch above the eleventh hole, shots overplayed to the right fall well down the hill leaving an awkward recovery pitch. With the strong wind coming in off the Atlantic, the player must start his ball well right to avoid having shots blow into the left side bunkers, fescue grasses, or the gorse covered slope.*

With as much as 18 hours of daylight during Dornoch summer days, few golfers will ever test this links just once in the day. It charms like few others because of its variety and the overall fun of playing its many intriguing holes. The wind blows hard here but rarely discourages players from trying Dornoch's many interesting shots. On a calm day, the course is far less interesting, but when the wind is up its subtly placed hazards and quirky contours become accentuated and require creative play.

With wind viewed so negatively in modern golf because it introduces elements of chance (in the eyes of some), C.B. Macdonald's writing on the positive impact of wind is still the best argument for its merits as a design aid: "Wind I consider the finest asset in golf; in itself it is one of the greatest and most delightful accompaniments in the game. Without wind your course is always the same, but as the wind varies in velocity and from the various points of the compass, you not only have one course but you have many courses."

Windy Day at Dornoch, Whinny Brae Hole

36 x 48, oil on panel, 1997 | Course: Royal Dornoch Golf Club, Dornoch, Scotland | Architects: Old Tom Morris, Donald Ross, George Duncan

Late Afternoon at Westward Ho!, The Crest Hole

36 x 48, oil on panel, 1999 | Course: Royal North Devon Golf Club, Devon, England | Architects: Mother Nature, Herbert Fowler

LATE AFTERNOON AT WESTWARD HO!, THE CREST HOLE: *Bernard Darwin said it best: "For fun and adventure of the game, there is no more ideal piece of golfing country in the world than Westward Ho!"*

Looking at this rendition of the 410-yard par-4 sixth, who can argue with the adventurous appeal of this two-shotter? If selected today for a new course to be built on this wondrous site overlooking the Atlantic, in all likelihood the sixth would not appear as it does here. The architect would be ordered to flatten out most of these contours to make the hole play more "fair" on the many windy days at Royal North Devon Golf Club (the formal title for this ancient links).

Thankfully, though, this land was used for golf as early as the mid-1800s and since its official founding in 1864, the golf club is the oldest continuously active one in England. Though revisions were made in 1908 by Herbert Fowler, the real architect here is Mother Nature.

Mike Miller took some artistic liberty with this painting by not including the sheep that "mow" the grass at Westward Ho! to this day. Miller also left out the unattractive orange tape used to keep the course's mowing crew off the greens, tape that only comes down for major competitions.

On the subject of luck and wind, no hole better reminds us of the variety and unpredictability of links golf, a charm that Bobby Jones felt was lacking from the American version of golf. He wrote, "Employing a comparison with our own best courses in America I have found that most of our courses, especially those inland, may be played correctly the same way round after round. The holes really are laid out scientifically; visibility is stressed; you can see what you have to do virtually all the time; and when once you learn how to do it, you can go right ahead, the next day, and the next day, and the day after that."

THE CAPE HOLE AT THE NATIONAL, CIRCA 2000: *The original version of Macdonald's "Cape" was a 305-yard par 4 with a green situated far to the right of this version, perched atop Bull Head's Bay. Macdonald constantly tinkered with his dream course, believing that "a first class course can only be made in time. It must develop. The proper distance between holes, the shrewd placing of bunkers and other hazards, the perfecting of putting greens, all must be evolved by a process of growth and it requires study and practice."*

In this case, the original club entrance road went through the middle of the course and became an annoyance, so Macdonald moved the road to the side of the fourteenth, forcing the new green to be built. The hole is longer today and the green is still guarded by water, though not as dramatically as the original. Still the undulating fairway will cause plenty of problems for the player attempting to approach this large green. Add the shifting winds off the bay and the exposed nature of the green, and the Cape provides plenty of subtle challenge. Of course, it is also believed Macdonald moved the fourteenth green because he didn't like players driving the hole in certain wind conditions.

Macdonald said of wind, "In designing a course try to lay out your holes so that they vary in direction. In this way a player gets an opportunity to play all the varying wind shots in a round. The National is noted for this. There is no wind from any point of the compass which favors a player for more than four or five holes."

The Cape Hole at the National, circa 2000

36 x 48, oil on panel, 2001 | Course: The National Golf Links of America, Southampton, New York | Architects: Charles Blair Macdonald and Seth Raynor

...we should revere the cradle of golf with its fine spirit and distinct atmosphere; but we may also be proud of our own development, and strive not only to keep up the standards of our past, but to go on and improve our newer productions, for the ultimate in golf and golf architecture is not yet attained...The question of strategy is of the utmost importance to the golf architect and to the golfer, and such strategy will be developed more and more during the coming years.

GEORGE C. THOMAS JR., 1927

What Happened to the Revolution?

During the first 30 years of the twentieth century, architecture was at its most creative with visionary designers like Alister MacKenzie and George Thomas predicting that the future would spawn even greater advancement in course design. They believed that architects would be wiser, better trained, and more daring. They also felt that the combination of improved construction techniques along with a better-educated golfing public would allow for widespread design work that was strategically complex and natural.

Surely the Old Course at St. Andrews was on their mind when predicting that strategy and construction would outdate their own work. They were surely envisioning the Old Course's features when stating that future courses would be able to present greater thinking tests while redefining subtlety, naturalness, and the genuine "sporting" spirit that results from a more unpredictable battle with nature. These masters envisioned everyday courses amplifying the complexities and artful contours that make the Old Course a new adventure every time out. And these great early twentieth century architects believed there eventually would be a well-educated mass of golfers who would lead the revolution. Because the average golfer would soon understand the beauty of a rugged-looking but strategically-sophisticated course, while rejecting geometric and strategically-challenged designs.

MacKenzie, Thomas, and Bobby Jones in particular, were fascinated by the constant variety the Old Course offered. But they were also disturbed by the lack of daily playing variety found in American courses. After all, each of the Golden Age architects said variety was a coveted characteristic in golf design and each emphasized the need for the kind of variety that keeps the game fresh and adventurous. The variety we speak of here is not found in some sort of systematic breakdown of holes and their yardages. But instead, in the mixture of decisions, shots, and conditions the player faces from round to round.

Thomas attempted to create "four courses within the

course" during his redesign of Los Angeles Country Club's North layout in 1927-28, his last significant design project (he later did the design for Stanford University Golf Course, but never visited the site). Thomas envisioned at least four primary interchangeable layouts at LACC with more possibilities existing if necessary. The many options ranged from a short par-69 design to an overwhelming par-73, 7,000-yard layout, all easily interchangeable on a day-to-day basis thanks to multiple hole and tee locations. Costwise, Thomas's concept only required that a few more auxiliary tees be constructed than normally needed, and no extra greens were necessary. For the concept to work, however, Thomas did need to add square footage to the greens for extra hole location options.

An avid sport fisherman, Thomas believed his concept might present the ultimate in variety to the club player who sought adventure—similar to that experienced by the patient sport fisherman who ultimately outwits his opponent. Thomas also believed that daily variety in golf courses would become the accepted method for setting up tournament courses because variance would reward the player most able to adapt to unfamiliar shots and decision-making circumstances.

However, none of Thomas's "revolutionary" ideas has been carried out in the years since his death. In fact, tournament golf and everyday golf have moved in the opposite direction, with a focus on consistency and sameness to the point players complain if tees are moved much from day-to-day.

Alister MacKenzie outlined multiple strategic routes in his early renderings of Augusta National. He and Bobby Jones believed that despite the course's less flexible inland setting among the pines, that wide fairways would make for reasonably "playable" holes for the average man. This width and the large greens they created at Augusta would invite careless play

by some. But if carefully planned out, their alternate playing routes at Augusta National would reward intelligent planning and execution by the shrewd player who placed themselves in the best positions to attack the hole. Like George Thomas, Jones and MacKenzie believed multiple avenues to the hole and the chance to have numerous hole locations provided the ultimate in variety and unexpected thrills for the adventuresome golfer.

The advancement of golf architecture, they believed, would also see progression in the construction and presentation of courses. All of the masters were fascinated by the concept of making golf courses look and play as natural as possible. They were intrigued by the idea of making the quest to the hole as mysterious and authentic as one could find in natural pursuits such as hunting or fishing (minus the macabre aspects of those sports). Many master golf architects hinted that in time, construction practices would become so refined that designers could transform properties into beautiful, ultrarustic settings that barely resembled a golf course. But once on its fairways, these layouts would feel like the ultimate battle against nature, with hardly any hint that man had altered the terrain to create strategic situations for golf.

So they understandably thought that such tantalizing and interesting design possibilities would become commonplace and would even be expanded on by future architects.

It never occurred.

What happened to the design revolution that MacKenzie, Thomas, and others foresaw?

Courses today have less variety and subtle strategy than ever before. Play is nearly always expected to be down the center, and if a course is not set up to the predictable "norms" as seen the last time the player drove around the course being guided by a Globally Positioned Satellite, the player feels something is amiss. And with regard to the "minimalist" or natural construction of layouts, there have been a few examples of the almost unimaginable naturalness that MacKenzie envisioned becoming common. Bill Coore and Ben Crenshaw's Sand Hills may be the ultimate example of the kind of subtle construction and strategic golf that Thomas and MacKenzie dreamed would be commonplace by now.

For the most part, however, the definition of "natural looking" in golf today is far from what MacKenzie envisioned. Mounding is rarely carried out with any effort to replicate natural features. Overmanicured bunkers and native areas never look as natural or irregular as they should. Waterfalls and concrete-lined lakes are too common in modern golf. And nothing looks more contrived than the introduction of concrete on a golf course.

Why did Golden Age standards cease?

The Great Depression and World War II put a stop to most course construction and helped cause the closing of many other existing courses. This trying time all but ended the careers of the Golden Age architects still living. Thus the torch was not passed along to the next group of aspiring architects, a group who ultimately sought to create their own distinct styles once course construction finally restarted on a widespread basis in the 1950s.

When the country got back on its feet, it was a more philosophically conservative world that was growing at a dizzying pace. Understandably, there was an underlying backlash toward the Roaring Twenties whose excesses were viewed by some as having gotten America in the mess it was in, particularly the events of October 1929. Also in the postwar era, America was expanding quickly and talent was spread thin.

Thus, many in the course construction and design business were not the artisans that their predecessors were.

The creative side of design often suffered in the name of rapid expansion, just as it did in pursuits such as building architecture or land planning. Function at its most basic level was the priority. Clever and ingenious design touches were not necessary, seemingly viewed as a waste of someone's time. There was little energy or room for discussion that would encourage something other than the bland styles being put forth by the "name architects" of the era. Large earthmoving equipment became available to make design work easier and faster. It was usually employed carelessly with little regard for mimicking the lines of nature.

Another mind-set crept into postwar golf that discouraged any expansion of Golden Age design principles. The courses of the previous decades were viewed as too wide and too easy, perhaps because they had rewarded the skills of players such as Hogan, Snead, and Nelson with birdies. Par, length, and straight play became the new "perceived" standard of excellence worth "protecting," even at the expense of the architecture.

The USGA's 1951 preparation of Robert Trent Jones's redesigned Oakland Hills became the acclaimed standard for golf course setup. Why?

Was it because it could be labeled "hard but fair" due to Hogan's brilliant 67 in the final round? (Had Hogan or another big name not won, would the course setup have been seen for what it was, over the top?) Eleven-time major winner Walter Hagen, then a retired but still wise observer of the game, summed the Oakland Hills penal setup best when he said, "The course is playing the players, not the players playing the course."

The new setup style reasoned that straight play down narrow corridors would reward the best talent. The concept of decision-making that was asked of the player in strategic design, or a variety of different "looks" presented by the architect, became concepts lost in outer space. Width was a bad thing and the narrow fairway a good thing because it eliminated the possibility of embarrassingly low scoring while still being "fair." The new approach stretched Oakland Hills like a rubber band, making it longer and tougher but also decreasing the width for play as the band stretched.

This rubber band approach to stretching and tightening courses expanded into mainstream golf as new bent grasses and the desire for lushness quickly became conventional and expected. To create bright green bent fairways, only irrigated areas could attain the lush look. So to save money and time, fairways were narrowed on everyday courses as well as on classic gems (even where the architecture dictated that width was key to their design). Trees were planted in the areas where fairway once existed. This was designed to further the narrowing effect and place that all-important premium on accuracy with little regard for the character of the original architect's vision.

To this day, those in charge of course setup do not realize that you make the game simpler for good players by telling them *how* to play a hole and where *not* to go. Good players get in much more trouble when there is room to hang themselves, room to consider aggressive attacks of the hole. They struggle when there are fewer road signs telling them where to play and where not to play. This type of subtlety leads to thinking. When players have to make decisions, they receive a greater test and we are more likely to separate the outstanding from the merely good.

As Wethered and Simpson pointed out in *The Architectural Side of Golf*, "When the unexpected confronts a man he is liable to be in two minds over the matter and is in danger of losing accuracy…mental balance is a matter of exceedingly delicate adjustment; and the true object of every game worthy of the name is to apply a test of the most searching kind possible in order to distinguish the superiority of one player over another. Without such a test a game would be scarcely worth the effort."

The Masters demonstrated the beauty of this kind of "mental balance" up through 1998, before the club started dismantling Jones and MacKenzie's design vision with rough and little pines planted to discourage aggressive and intelligent play. What also is missed today (but was clearly understood by the master architects) was that this kind of wide, thought-provoking setup is not overly exhausting for the average player who has to test the course the other 51 weeks of the year.

Since the postwar penal setup approach to tournament courses, the notion of variety in American golf has slowly died. A course is not normal if it is anything but par 70, 71, or 72. And a layout is not really of championship quality unless its yardage is over 6,700 yards, preferably pushing or topping 7,000 yards. Blind shots, offbeat holes, extremely short holes and—heaven forbid—a hole that does NOT give you a road map on how to play it, are all considered design anomalies today. One "signature" hole, surrounded by 17 "pretty but fair" siblings is considered acceptable architecture.

In other words, stroke play and "fairness" take priority over the elements that make certain courses special. Elements such as drama, suspense, variety, and fun. And it's all in the name of protecting a course from an "embarrassing" low score or to ensure that most players do not suffer the awful misfortune of poor luck.

Unpredictability, cleverness, mystery, chance, and the ability to laugh it all off when the day is done—the elements that help define play on the Old Course—are simply not part of golf anymore. Sameness, perfect visibility, no "rub of the green," and no surprises are the priority now, and frankly, it's a boring version of the adventurous sport that originated in Scotland. It also goes against the American spirit of being bold, courageous, and original.

The combination of all these strong forces working against the ideas of the master architects makes it seemingly impossible to envision a contemporary design revolution occurring. Can you imagine the average club member walking out to their course one day to play George Thomas's par-73, 7,000 yard monster with holes cut in reasonably easy places, only to return the next day to see the superintendent had set up the course as a wily par-69 at 5,900 yards, with several tucked hole locations and never-before encountered club selection decisions on each hole? And to return for yet a third day to find a course setup somewhere in between the two? It couldn't happen in today's version of golf. If the superintendent pulled such a "stunt," he would soon be unemployed.

American golfers have been taught to demand predictability and a sameness to their golf, which stifles their long-term interest in the game. Though they likely won't know why golf has grown dull to them.

Is there any glimmer of hope for a design revolution, or should the goal in our lifetime simply be to see a return to the basics of tempting, original design? Is merely reintroducing basic strategy, a little charm, width, some originality, and construction artistry the lone goal?

Golfers may not know it, but playing the same course and the same holes the same way eventually takes the genuine joy out of the game. Sure it seems comforting at first, but this kind of predictability wears thin. If the game gets stale, its cost, its difficulty, and the time it takes to play eventually scares people off. This is why, despite a booming economy, Tiger Woods's mainstream influence, and more well-maintained courses to choose from than ever, golf has only seen growth by a couple of million players in the last 20 years of the twentieth century. Meanwhile, according to the National Golf Foundation there are an estimated 41 million who would like to play but who are opting to stay on the sidelines because there are too many issues scaring them off and not enough good reasons to take up golf. This is where golf architecture and development has let the game down, and why we so sorely miss the revolution that never occurred.

Dynamic architecture can be the single most original and distinctive element of golf and the best tool the game has for spawning growth in unimaginable ways. The groundwork laid by the early architects and the Old Course has been wasted. The British model of fun, natural, and affordable community courses has never been accepted in America. Short holes and short courses are considered "weak" by many golfers and are supposedly only for beginners. So no one builds them. And if they do, their architecture almost always fails to inspire.

Sure, design and course construction have improved, particularly on the scientific side (by creating more maintainable courses). But the cost and extravagance of design, and even—some would say—the extreme overemphasis on function to the point of banality, have failed to provide the elements of strategy and variety that ultimately enamor new golfers or keep longtime ones sticking around.

If an architect took a flat piece of land near a body of water with shifting winds, and took the time to build a course with the kind of strategy and wild contours found on the Old Course, the place wouldn't stand a chance. Sure, the purists would try it out and a local population would support it if their alternatives were limited. But few would care for it or have the patience to discover its nuances. Most would find its quirkiness downright offensive.

The complex but ultimately fascinating strategy and naturalness that the classic architects envisioned requires thought and even a little anguish to figure out. But there is apparently no room in the game for that kind of variety today. Predictability, sameness, and fairness rule golf. Tour players are considered the leading authorities on design. Yet you know how they judge a course, don't you?

By how fair it is. How it fits their game. How visually perfect it is. (Typical modern PGA Tour player design praise: "I love this course because everything is right in front of you and it really fits my game.")

If a course makes them think or forces them to try a shot they don't normally hit "on Tour," there is something peculiar about the place (because its unusual twists are interfering with their ability to make a living without thought).

Of course there wasn't room for much complexity in architecture around 1928 either. But the daring spirit that prevailed during the '20s did leave room for creativity on the architect's behalf, and discussion of course design was more prevalent than it is today. Still, visionaries such as MacKenzie and Thomas and Tillinghast and Behr pushed the limit. They went to great lengths to educate golfers about the possibilities. They lured golfers in with their beautiful looking and playable designs, then injected strategy to accentuate the beauty they worked so hard to sculpt.

However, in their hearts they hoped that there would come a day when they would not have to build such straightforward-looking holes in order to lure the golfers. They genuinely believed a less forthright looking but more thought-provoking and ruggedly beautiful design would fascinate golfers. And that the next generation of architects would take their ideas and expand on them.

But this does not mean certain influential people with certain tastes can't at least dream of the possibilities and even try to carry some of them out.

It would be a start.

And a start is all you need to spark a revolution.

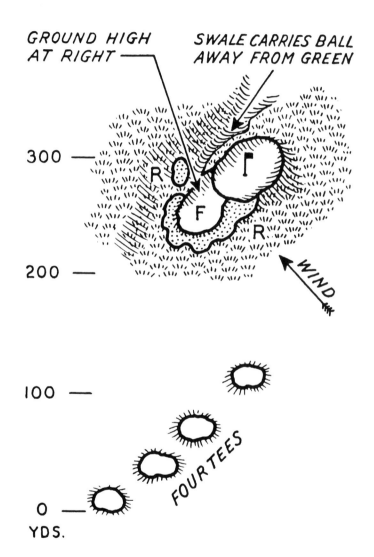

SKETCH BY THOMAS OF LACC'S ELEVENTH: *George Thomas's original drawing of the eleventh at Los Angeles Country Club North. This is one of many holes where Thomas envisioned his "four courses within the course" at LACC, the idea being that the hole could be played any number of ways depending on the setup style for that particular day. It was Thomas's suggestion to introduce that kind of variety to design in order to take the game to new levels architecturally.*

Of all the holes at this fine layout, the eleventh may have been the most interesting in Thomas's scheme. The long par 3 that it plays as today is a strong one and a thrilling shot to attempt carrying off, yet played at 300 yards as a short par 4 on occasion, the hole becomes one of a totally different nature without any necessary changes to the green complex. As a short two-shotter, either the player can drive the green, or lay up and face an uphill, semiblind pitch shot. And on days when the superintendent felt like giving the player a different look, the tee could be placed well forward and the cup located close to the bunkers. But such daring, spontaneous spirit in the modern game is frowned upon. Any superintendent who would mix up the playing distances of a hole such as this would probably lose his job for daring to add zest and variety to the game. Such a misunderstanding for the charm in this kind of day-to-day variety explains why the "revolution" that Thomas and others foresaw has never taken shape.

ELEVENTH AT LOS ANGELES COUNTRY CLUB NORTH, CIRCA 1929: *Shown here on a typical spring day in Southern California, the eleventh at Los Angeles Country Club's North Course was a prime example of George Thomas's concept of creating the ultimate in variety within one course. He believed it might lead to a revolution in how designers could create vastly different playing possibilities on a day-to-day basis. The eleventh was primarily a 244-yard, par 3, with some playing characteristics of a Redan par 3, only reversed to reward a left-to-right play. But Thomas also designed a 300-yard tee to create a high risk driveable par 4 for the strong player. The bunkering and green contours were designed to make a challenging pitch for those who laid up if playing it as a two-shotter. Thomas envisioned this option as an intriguing alternative during tournament play or simply when players wanted a fresh way to play a hole. A final option was to play the hole as a short par 3, from the area just to the right of where Miller's image is depicted.*

As a member of Los Angeles Country Club and an architect who offered his services for free, Thomas had his fellow members' long-term playing interest at heart, and he believed that such stark variety would keep the game fresh for his friends at the club and, eventually, throughout golf. Mike Miller's depiction of the bunkering created by Thomas and Billy Bell during a 1928 renovation of the course reminds us that these architects were masters of both strategy and construction artistry in golf architecture.

Eleventh at Los Angeles Country Club North, circa 1929

24 x 26, oil on panel, 1999 | Course: The Los Angeles Country Club North Course, Los Angeles, California | Architects: George C. Thomas Jr. and Billy Bell

Riviera's Sixteenth, Summer Afternoon, circa 1997

36 x 48, oil on pane, 1998 | Course: Riviera Country Club, Los Angeles, California | Architects: George C. Thomas Jr. and Billy Bell.

RIVIERA'S SIXTEENTH, SUMMER AFTERNOON, CIRCA 1997: *Besides Thomas's desire to see multiple strategic options for holes, he also believed that creating extra tees would help solve functional dilemmas as well. On Riviera's sixteenth, players approaching this green in the lovely late afternoons in Santa Monica Canyon are nearly always faced with the setting sun. So Thomas created tees well left and right of the main tee to be used for the extreme times of year. This would allow golfers to watch their ball and not worry about being blinded by the setting sun. It also lent variety to the everyday play of this magnificently bunkered short par 3, of 168 yards, shown here after years of play and evolution.*

This combination of function and variety is another victim of golf architecture's dark years. Such a simple, interesting concept should be par for course construction today as a result of having been passed down by previous generations. Or in the view of Thomas and MacKenzie, perhaps even refined and expanded on as a design concept. But instead, it was lost and an architect attempting to create such a solution today would probably be considered a bit odd.

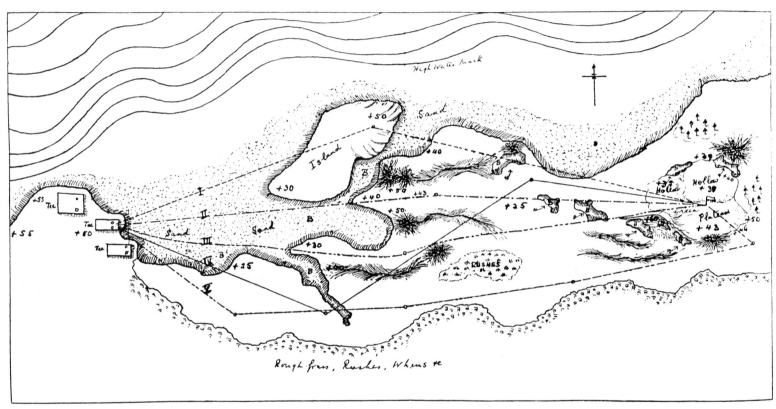

THE FIRST PRIZE DESIGN OF A TWO-SHOT HOLE, BY DR. A. MACKENZIE
Which won a golfing architecture competition in England for three prizes given by Mr. C. B. Macdonald

MacKenzie's "Lido" Prize Rendering

MACKENZIE'S "LIDO" PRIZE RENDERING: *Alister MacKenzie won* Country Life Magazine's *"Lido" Prize in 1914. The hole MacKenzie designed on paper was constructed in modified form by C.B. Macdonald and Seth Raynor at the Lido Golf Club on Long Island. The complex strategy and multiple playing routes were well ahead of their time and surely a style of architecture MacKenzie learned from the Old Course at St. Andrews, and perhaps envisioned as the future of golf design.*

SUN SETTING BEHIND THE EIGHTEENTH AT PASATIEMPO, CIRCA 1929: *Alister MacKenzie's "bleeding bunkers" at Pasatiempo demonstrate his desire to build more dynamic and natural looking courses. The two front bunkers on this thrilling one-shotter were added after the course was complete, and have since disappeared after washing away into the canyon that is so carefully depicted here by Mike Miller. The green setting also demonstrates MacKenzie's talent for not only creating beauty, but holes filled with a variety of playing choices. Hole locations ranged dramatically from the back-left to the front-right. Depending on green speeds and the status of a match, the differing hole locations could tempt players to either try for a daring play onto the precipices created by MacKenzie, or play safer shots to the middle and back of the putting surface. Though par 3s are not necessarily ideal finishing holes, Alister MacKenzie managed to put a remarkable amount of interest and artistry into this classic hole of 135 yards. The Santa Cruz, California, course was opened in 1929 as part of a development by Marion Hollins.*

MacKenzie wrote in 1934, "Golf architecture is a new art closely allied to that of the artist or sculptor, but also necessitating a scientific knowledge of many other subjects. The modern designer...is likely to achieve the most perfect results and make the fullest use of all the natural features by more up-to-date methods."

Sun Setting behind the Eighteenth at Pasatiempo, circa 1929

36 x 48, oil on panel, 1998 | Course: Pasatiempo Golf Club, Santa Cruz, California | Architect: Alister MacKenzie

The Approach to Cypress Point's Thirteenth, circa 1929

36 x 48, oil on panel, 2000 | Course: Cypress Point Club, Pebble Beach, California | Architects: Alister MacKenzie and Robert Hunter

THE APPROACH TO CYPRESS POINT'S THIRTEENTH, CIRCA 1929: *Arguably as close to perfection as MacKenzie and Hunter came in building natural looking hazards, the thirteenth green at Cypress Point surely demonstrates MacKenzie's vision for the future of course construction—hazards that "bleed" into the landscape as if they were found and merely made functional for play. They are also hazards that astound in their beauty and yet do not "stick out" in any kind of offensive way, but instead, embellish the landscape and lend drama to the front hole locations. As noted earlier in this book, these bunkers were a "last-minute" creation. Photos of the course before its opening show that the dunes surrounding the green were still in their raw state. But at some point, the ridge protecting the left-rear of the green was converted into bunkering—perhaps for a functional purpose, such as preventing the dunes from eroding. More likely, it was done for aesthetics.*

The attractive bunker short-left of the green was always intended to be a hazard and though it appears to rest fairly close to the green, it actually sits well short of the putting surface. Tee shots that play to the safer left side of the fairway result in a second shot over this bunker. It is extremely difficult to gauge the distance here, particularly with winds coming off the Pacific Ocean, which sits only 75 yards from this stunning green complex.

Robert Hunter, who supervised construction on this wondrous course and was influential in its design, also believed the art of design would be taken to new "revolutionary" levels. He wrote in 1926, "...even better work will be done in the future. We are still in the infancy of this art. The better work being done at present and the steadily improving standard of all work in this field speaks well for the future."

THE RUGGED BUNKERING OF KINGSTON HEATH: *Even though MacKenzie's trip to Australia in 1926 was brief, the ability to effectively communicate his unique design ideas made a permanent impression on Australian golf design. MacKenzie came to Australia at the request of the Royal Melbourne Golf Club, but his commission to redesign Kingston Heath has made just as strong an impression on the game as his brilliant 36 holes at Melbourne. Kingston Heath had an existing, bunkerless Dan Souter design built in the early 1920s. MacKenzie filed a report suggesting the addition of the famous bunkers we come to know as the modern Kingston Heath, along with an entirely new par 3. That hole was the 156-yard fifteenth, portrayed here in a vertical rendition by Miller. This famous one-shotter features an enormous carry bunker starting just off the tee and running to within a few yards of the green. From there, the tightly bunkered putting surface features more dramatic hazards.*

Golfing great Peter Thomson, now an architect and passionate observer of Australian golf, wrote these interesting remarks about MacKenzie, golf architecture, and Kingston Heath:

"The 15th is not a hole for the fainthearted. In concept it is brilliant. Of just 142 meters, uphill, the hole asks for bull's-eye accuracy. The consequences of missing the target can be very expensive. The bunkers are extensive and cavernous. One can imagine the terror they must have struck in the early days before the invention of the round soled sand iron. Trying to escape from these with a sharp edged niblick must have led to many a torn up card! Even with modern implements the shots demanded from the bunkers are of the highest skill, especially if the sand is soft. Not many attempters 'get down in two.' The green itself is small in size and is tilted steeply from back to front. The feature is enough to cause trembles.

"In my formative years my eye became accustomed to the MacKenzie look. I came to recognize the merit of his design. I became a believer in his philosophy of the game, as it applies to the golf holes. He intended holes to be 'enjoyable,' 'tempting,' free from irritations and torment, and certainly free from the 'humbug of lost balls.' This was not just the Scotsman in him coming through. It makes the soundest common sense - just as much today as it did half a century ago. There is a real art to golf architecture. It involves many skills and gifts. It is a tradesman's job that produces a course that makes Greg Norman's knees shake. Almost anyone can do that. It is another matter to design a course that is all things to all manner of golfers."

The Rugged Bunkering of Kingston Heath

48 x 36, oil on panel, 2000 | Course: Kingston Heath Golf Club, Melbourne, Australia | Architects: Alister MacKenzie and Alex Russell

I cannot help being saddened by what you tell me of the changes in turf conditions at Lytham. I know I was shocked to observe the same changes at St. Andrews. If this sort of thing is happening to all British seaside golf, then indeed, progress has been dearly bought...I am happy now that I did not miss playing seaside golf when the greens were hard and unwatered and the fairways and putting surfaces like glass. Nothing resulting from man-made design can equal the testing qualities of such conditions.

BOBBY JONES, 1961 LETTER TO PAT WARD-THOMAS

Progress Dearly Bought?

Without the design revolution discussed in the previous chapter, other elements vital to the health of golf architecture never "progressed" as the master architects might have envisioned. The art form known as golf course design is not dead, but it certainly has not progressed.

The most notable areas failing to advance the spirit of the "revolution" would be in maintenance, course setup, and the disappearance of certain design quirks. Even worse, the Great Depression and World War II resulted in drastic changes to numerous wonderful 1920s designs, prompting the question, has progress been dearly bought? Such a query cannot be fairly answered without delving into specific questions.

When has a course aged gracefully and when has it deteriorated?

What happened to so many "lost" courses, and are we missing out on some true classics?

How much has the improved maintenance of courses furthered the quality of the game that the visionaries of the early century left behind, and is course setup stifling creative and skillful play?

The first question is the most subjective, but in general most of our classic courses have not aged gracefully. The majority, while still being worthy of classic status, have deteriorated in ways that would never be tolerated in other art forms.

Accepting that all courses will evolve due to play, maintenance and weather, it is safe to generalize that all but a handful of the most timeless designs have seen the addition of too many trees choking landing areas. They've had too many bunkers filled in that once served an interesting, attractive purpose. And most of their greens have lost key hole locations due to careless mowing patterns or evolving bunkers.

The recent restoration movement has tried and often struggled to convince those in charge of classic courses to recapture their once larger greens, wider fairways, and lost hazards. When architects have tried to expand greens and take out trees in order to reopen old strategic avenues, the regulars at such courses cry that the courses are being made too easy. When the architects attempt to restore lost bunkers or other hazards, the same players cry that the course is being made too difficult for the average player and such restoration is not only unnecessary, but actually cruel to the weaker players.

This kind of meddling by members at supposed "tradition-based" golf clubs demonstrates why many modern architects capable of deferential restoration work simply stay away from efforts to bring back these masterworks. The architects understand the artistry of the original masters. However, no matter how many archival photographs they discover or sound reasons they can provide to restore the original canvas, less knowledgeable golfers seem to feel a need to interfere. So, lesser architects then step in with little understanding of what made the classic architecture unique and often make a greater mess by injecting their own style. In many cases these inferior architects will happily incorporate the membership's ideas, which are born out of the members own blatant self-interests with little appreciation for the overall artistry of the original design.

Most of the classic courses should be treated no differently than a Van Gogh painting or a Frank Lloyd Wright structure. Do you hire Leroy Neiman fresh off one of his African safaris to restore "Starry, Starry Night?" No, as he would probably be inclined to introduce his own style since he is a major commercial artist, not a restorer. And you don't try to hire the eccentric modern architect Frank Gehry to restore a Wright prairie house simply because he is the en vogue architect of his generation and you prefer the twisting pile of bronze that is the Guggenheim Museum.

You restore these classic golf courses because they are masterworks. If you want hip, cutting-edge, or just plain modern, then build a new layout and leave the old ones to those who want to experience classic golf architecture.

This is not to preach that a dramatic restoration is always the best idea. There are a few notable examples of classic courses which were extraordinary soon after their completion and remain so today despite dramatic changes that may not reflect the architect's original vision.

The most engaging example of this class of evolution is Pebble Beach Golf Links. Redesigned in 1928 by noted amateur golfer H. Chandler Egan, the two-time U.S. Amateur Champion transformed a 10-year old course from a crude, geometrically shaped and strategically-challenged design into a bold combination of ultranatural dunes and thinking man's architecture.

Egan's bold work may have been in an effort to keep up with Alister MacKenzie's neighboring Cypress Point design, which was constructed at the same time Pebble Beach received its 1928 "facelift." And interestingly, MacKenzie's American Golf Course Construction Company was handling the work for both courses.

In order to make Pebble Beach stand out against the impressive competition just up Seventeen Mile Drive, Egan opted to create man-made "imitation sand dunes" on the Pebble Beach course, a concept no one had ever tried in golf course design. As remarkable as they were the imitation dunes apparently became impractical to maintain over the years. As the fierce weather continued to blow sand away and create a maintenance nightmare, the dunes were eventually turned into bunkers by various course superintendents. With Pebble Beach getting upward of 70,000 rounds a year during the 1980s, the bunkers then evolved substantially on their own, thanks to flying sand and increased maintenance.

Many view the disappearance of the imitation dunes as a defeat for artistic design and the loss of one of golf architecture's boldest endeavors. Perhaps that's true, but Chandler Egan's *strategic* design influence remains intact with only the shrinkage of green square footage taking away from his original concepts. Otherwise, the course contains the same captivating, contemplative elements that Egan injected, minus the imitation dunes.

Is this progress? No.

Is it progress dearly bought? Certainly not.

This is merely the evolution of a great course and a rare example of a layout metamorphosing while preserving its most timeless design characteristic: sound strategy. Sure, some of the architect's original colors are lost and the canvas is a little beaten up, but the soul of his original work is still very much intact. A similar case could be made for William Flynn's Shinnecock Hills, which once featured vast sandy areas and several holes with as many as 30 bunkers—areas that have now been overtaken by native fescue grasses, but the strategy remains.

When further delving into the issue of progress, the most unfortunate change we have seen in golf is in the number of great courses lost. In particular, the collection of wonderfully designed public-access courses by the master architects.

It is extremely rare that the average daily-fee paying customer gets to play a course designed by Tillinghast, Ross, Colt, MacKenzie, or Thomas, all of whom created renowned public designs. When the public course player does get to test one of their creations, the design is usually in such depleted form as to be unrecognizable to the architect if he showed up there today.

Most of these public-access course gems (and quite a few private club designs as well) disappeared during the Great Depression and World War II. Though the dire circumstances make their closure understandable, it is disturbing what happened when life returned to normal and golf boomed in the 1950s. Many courses reopened on the same sites as these architectural gems. However, in nearly all cases, the previous designs were not returned to a state even resembling their previous appearance. Architects injected their own ideas and seemed to go out of their way to ignore what existed previously. Private clubs that survived the lean years also were known to distance themselves from the architecture of the previous generation in favor of more sterile and penal designs.

We will never understand why there was so little vision or respect for the pre-Depression period of design during those postwar years. Perhaps it was just the rapid-growing nature of the postwar society and the desire to forget the extravagances of the "Roaring Twenties." However, this era of important layouts either never coming back or returning to service in a disfigured state forever changed the public's perception of golf architecture's potential. Moreover, it eliminated the chance for the majority of golfers to experience masterful works as the architect envisioned them. In the case of missing links such as Timber Point in New York and Fox Hills in California, and many others once available to all golfers, progress has been dearly bought.

The final question in debating progress or a lack thereof in architecture involves the issue of golf course maintenance. Accompanying that is the impact of improved course maintenance on strategy, the extra cost required to create certain "looks" and expectations the average player now has for "ideal" playing conditions.

As Bobby Jones pointed out in the letter cited at the beginning of this essay, he was disappointed to see what had happened to the maintenance of links courses when he returned to Scotland in 1958. Jones was not criticizing the work of the superintendents nor was he attempting to demean the Scots (he adored them). But Jones agreed with noted writer Pat Ward-Thomas that the sport had changed for the worse due to overirrigation. He strongly believed that softer turf conditions had taken away key sporting elements in golf. Much of what Jones referred to goes back to the notion of golf being a battle against nature as opposed to a battle against the hand of man. Jones bemoaned the modern desire to take scientific control of everything—including golf clubs, on-course thinking, and maintenance—because he believed it robbed the game of certain thrills.

A sense of challenge and accomplishment is derived from occasionally playing off uneven, natural surfaces and finding the inner strength to overcome odd lies, penal bunkers, and firm ground. But as difficult as that is, golfers such as Jones understood that those challenges were far more satisfying to overcome than uniformly long rough, narrow fairways, and superficial obstacles. Jones also understood that the best golf was rewarded on firm and fast ground, not softer, slower conditions. He also believed that a genuinely good design would be better, appreciated in these conditions.

The average golfer, and even the cultivated student of design, will always prefer lush greenery over a course with a variety of "hues." No one will disagree that green is anything but soothing and wonderful to look at. And the modern day golf course superintendent is so talented and given such an arsenal of products to present consistent greenery that it would be professional suicide for them not to give the golfers what they want—even if it's at the expense of more traditional playing surfaces which accentuate the architecture

(i.e., firm, fast fairways and greens).

However, I would argue that superintendents and progressive technology are not completely to blame for the green effect in golf. Instead, it is an admixture of powerful forces that have combined to lead golf maintenance in a different direction. Those in charge are merely doing what is necessary to stay employed. Either way, it is a direction that in many cases has stripped the game of certain charms and also driven the price to play through the ceiling. And in the case of hazards, a cleaner look has eliminated many of the most attractive-looking bunkers and creeks in golf.

Though few would argue that we should step backward to circa 1925 playing conditions, it does seem that a balance must be found to present courses beautifully but naturally. An effort should be made to return firm and fast conditions as the way to reward great play over merely average play, and to stop relying on rough and the addition of trees to promote accuracy. An effort must be made to start blending courses into their surroundings to reflect genuine artistry by mirroring the surrounding environment and respecting that environment by using less water and fewer nonorganic fertilizers.

A failure to find a middle ground between pleasing maintenance and a natural appearance to courses will doom the development of future layouts because of cost and regulations. Environmentalists nearly always cite the audacious nature of courses that offends them more than the game itself. Among the real eyesores they cite as irritating: concrete lined lakes with large streaming fountains, blinding white bunker sand, lush greenery created by the use of damaging chemicals, and trees imported to nonnative surroundings. The misuse of water is always near the top of their lists as well.

Talk of maintenance also brings up the seldom understood

concept of how a course reflects the architect's vision. Are the holes maintained in a way that reflects their strategic playing possibilities? Is the bunkering presented in an irregular, natural looking state that the architect's crew worked hard to create?

Simple changes in mowing patterns, alterations to fairway contours, and decisions to stop maintaining certain areas can radically alter a course over time. More often than not, the changes are subtle and occur harmlessly, but their overall effect can be devastating to the artistry of a design.

The area most subtly affected by modern maintenance practices has been the green complex.

Over time, greens have "shrunk" and become more oval in shape, often losing the unique corner hole locations created by the original architect. Alister MacKenzie, A.W. Tillinghast, and George Thomas in particular, built larger, more irregularly shaped green boundaries than they are given credit for. C.B. Macdonald and Seth Raynor built enormous greens, many with "square fronts." But over time their green shapes have lost many engaging hole locations due to gradual changes in mowing patterns and a lack of attention to preserving the original green boundary lines. Many perceive them as builders of "small" greens, when quite the opposite is the case.

Changes in maintenance practices to the detriment of a course's architecture have even taken place at the best course in the world, Pine Valley. On their short par-4 seventeenth, an alternate fairway briefly provided a more testing, option laden tee shot. Playing to a blind area to the right rewarded the player with a better view of the putting surface, which is semi-blind from the primary left-hand fairway. Such an interesting risk-reward hole would be a fine addition to this masterpiece and perhaps, if feasible, the old fairway will return someday.

Why did the old fairway end up as a sea of native grasses and sand? In the early days of Pine Valley's existence they could not get a hose to reach far enough in order to water the alternate fairway, so the superintendent simply had to let it go.

This kind of seemingly minor and unintentional neglect has occurred all over the world with classic courses. Partly because golf courses are living, growing components of nature that are bound to change, but also because few have been viewed as the artistic masterpieces that they genuinely are. And when you are talking about a Pine Valley or a Cypress Point, maintenance dilemmas always must be secondary to preserving the architecture and treating these courses with the same care that museum curators treat their Monets or their Renoirs. With the development of the golf course superintendent as the most educated and talented of all golf course employees, the ability to balance quality maintenance with more intricate aesthetic touches meant to complement the architecture should be more possible than ever before.

In the area of championship course setup where progress genuinely has been dearly bought, an ironic approach has seeped into the mind-set of those preparing courses for tournament play. With golf equipment out of control and players stronger than ever, there is a knee-jerk reaction to stretch courses and even soften landing areas in order to "put long irons back into the players' hands." These longer approach shots are deemed to be in line with the same irons used by previous generations of golfers. Club members are afraid of players dominating their layout and thus do almost everything in their power to squelch the advantage of those talented enough to carry a ball 300 yards off the tee. Yet they never do the one thing that will address the power issue and reward the best players: return strategic elements to golf course setup.

Augusta National has been the most embarrassing example of a course with a vast inferiority complex. In recent years the powers that be have gone to great lengths to slow down drives and they even appear obsessed with statistical analysis to tell them how the course "held up." Their effort to take the subjective out of the game —the very concept that Bobby Jones so desperately injected into the design—has included mowing fairways toward tees, tucking in rough lines to eliminate certain angles to greens, and adding silly little trees to block off optional avenues to holes. But it has done nothing to serve the game in a positive manner or present the Masters as Bobby Jones envisioned it.

With improved maintenance practices and more talented individuals maintaining courses, the ability to manipulate grasses and hazards has never been greater. But as we've seen over and over again, the more man tries to interfere with the playing of golf through the use of extreme setups, the more contrived things get. And the less interesting the golf becomes to play or watch.

Progress is not tricking up a course to keep scores "in line with the past" or out of double-digit red figures. Progress certainly does not entail attempts to control players or influence the outcome of golf matches. But progress does entail setting up a course to reward shrewd play, not prevent it.

Improvements in the science of golf course maintenance and the game in general necessitate finding a balance between enjoyable turf conditions and firm, natural situations that reward sound thinking and precise play. Such conditions would also restore the game to its traditional roots by complementing the environment and giving the player a unique battle against Mother Nature's most charming and often unpredictable elements. The object should not be to make tournament golf a fight against the most manipulative setup man can muster to prevent a 300-yard drive or the dreaded birdie.

Progress in golf architecture depends on a better understanding from golfers of reasonable maintenance standards and sound implementation of course care practices. Progress also means a keener understanding of what constitutes positive evolution in courses and detrimental changes to the architect's artistic touch. Until that understanding can be reached, progress has and will continue to be, as Bobby Jones stated in 1961, dearly bought.

What Are We Missing?

BY DANIEL WEXLER

The two great rushes of American golf course construction have been well chronicled, the first during the game's pre-WWII Golden Age, the second still in full flight as we enter the new millennium. But this long-term expansion of the game's playing fields has not been a one-way street. Indeed, literally hundreds of layouts have disappeared from the American landscape since the onset of the Depression, the precise number of which we shall never truly know.

Many of these lost courses were rudimentary in nature; simple tracks routed across farms and private estates offering little in the way of strategy or excitement. Many others, however, were genuine beauties; fascinating, attractive designs created by the finest architects of the period. As a whole, the members of this latter group were generally comparable to many other Golden Age classics that remain in existence today. By departing from the scene prematurely, however, they seldom suffered the "renovations" that have pervaded the modern era and thus remain well-preserved in our mind's eyes in their strategic, highly-artistic original forms.

Perhaps no course answers to that description better than C.B. Macdonald's legendary Lido Golf Club in Lido Beach, NY. Pinched tightly between the waters of Reynolds Channel and the Atlantic Ocean, The Lido was golf's first truly man-made course; a good portion of its 115 acres comprised of landfill, virtually all of its contouring shaped by Seth Raynor's construction crew to Macdonald's whim. What resulted was a landscape largely British in appearance, its fairways flanked by thick rough, stands of beach grass and the cold, pounding waves of the Atlantic. Ever-present breezes and plentiful-but-quirky bunkering gave it decidedly links-like playing qualities. The fact that it was only photographed in black and white, often with wind howling and surf flying, only adds to that collective memory.

Another lost facility whose mix of strategy and beauty is sorely missed is Long Island's Timber Point, a C.H. Alison design utilizing perhaps the most varied American terrain this side of Cypress Point. On the front nine, parkland holes reminiscent of Wentworth or Woodhall Spa were followed by a more open heath-like stretch that recalled Sunningdale or Pine Valley. On the inward half, the routing proceeded through stark, largely man-made sand dunes, then down to the shoreline before sweeping back to the clubhouse with an eminently-reachable par-5 finisher. Remembering Timber Point (which technically still exists as a much-altered 27-hole facility) is to remember a layout of widely varied images, a marvelous tableau the likes of which modern architecture seems sadly unable to duplicate.

Of course for the average player, exposure to golf architecture—both good and bad—generally begins with public courses, and here the game has suffered losses of a different kind. Certainly from the most basic perspective, layouts like Dr. Alister MacKenzie's Bayside Links in New York, George Thomas's Fox Hills in California, and A.W. Tillinghast's Beaver Tail in Rhode Island, have vanished altogether. But less obvious is the sort of long-term, gradual decline (generally due to constrictive maintenance budgets) that has affected public-access and municipal facilities from coast to coast. The loss or modification of so many interesting holes and hazards has frequently resulted in public golf completely devoid of flair and style, with homogenously-shaped greens and bunkers and a focus far more upon dollars than any degree of strategy or style. Hardly the loss of golf courses in the strictest sense, but a loss of much of what is great about the game nonetheless.

CLEAR SUMMER DAY, SEVENTH AT PEBBLE BEACH, CIRCA 1929: *Egan's "imitation sand dunes" are in their full glory as seen in this depiction of Pebble Beach's 110-yard, par 3 in 1929. The dunes were created to transform Pebble Beach's then geometric bunkering into some of golf's most natural looking and difficult hazards.*

Chandler Egan's chance to "doctor" Pebble Beach did not officially come until December of 1927, when the course was awarded the 1929 United States Amateur after an exhaustive attempt to lobby the Eastern establishment within the USGA. It was the first time a major USGA event would be played west of Minneapolis, and came only after a strong campaign from Jack Neville, Roger Lapham, and Samuel Morse. Part of the USGA's suggestion for securing the Amateur was a course overhaul which they felt was needed to provide a better test for Bobby Jones and his fellow amateur contestants.

Egan wrote of his innovative bunkering: "Joe Mayo and I had never seen this type of bunkering done before but we had faith in the idea and after a few experiments achieved a result that we hope will continue to be as good as it seems at this writing."

With harsh weather and hard times all part of Pebble Beach's evolution, the imitation dunes bunkering did not last long. Eventually they evolved into bunkers with the help of various superintendents and architects. Though Egan's vision deteriorated without much chance to determine if the experiment could work, Pebble Beach's Egan-injected design strategy has remained and shines today.

Clear Summer Day, Seventh at Pebble Beach, circa 1929

36 x 48, oil on panel, 1997 | Course: Pebble Beach Golf Links | Architects: H. Chandler Egan (routing by Jack Neville and Douglas Grant)

Early Fall Day, Seventh at Pebble Beach, circa 1998

22 x 26 oil on panel, 1999 | Course: Pebble Beach Golf Links | Architects: H. Chandler Egan (routing by Jack Neville and Douglas Grant)

EARLY FALL DAY, SEVENTH AT PEBBLE BEACH, CIRCA 1998: *Seen here in its evolved state, the seventh remains one of the world's most beautiful and thrilling holes. Clean-edged bunkers now surround the green, yet they have taken on a certain character that is still attractive. Or as Wethered and Simpson once wrote, the bunkers still have a character that makes them hard to ignore. As they wrote in* The Architectural Side of Golf, *some bunkers just have a certain "vitality":*

"Vitality is another quality that is essential. Instinctively we feel that one course is alive, another dead and insipid, lacking energy of expression. We look for the unexpected note and a pleasantness of line. Every curve should have a spring in it, and no straight line should ever be quite straight. Generally the detection of these slight differences is purely a matter of feeling which once experienced is not likely to be forgotten."

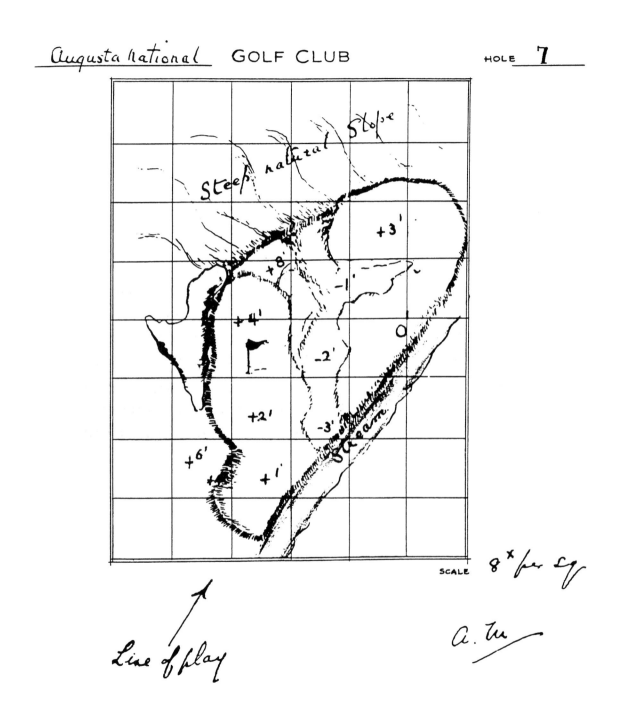

MacKenzie Rendering of Augusta National's Original Sixteenth Green

MACKENZIE RENDERING OF AUGUSTA NATIONAL'S ORIGINAL SIXTEENTH GREEN: *Drawn as the seventh hole but later switched to the sixteenth at Augusta National, MacKenzie stated that this green was inspired by the seventh at Stoke Pages in England. Even though his handwriting suggests the line of play was from the lower left angle, the primary tee used for this hole came from the area to the right, near the fifteenth green. The MacKenzie green was removed in 1947 and replaced with a longer version over a pond and to the right of this site.*

AUGUSTA NATIONAL'S SIXTEENTH, CIRCA 1932: *Until it was removed in 1947 and replaced by a new par 3 that was designed in part by Bobby Jones, the original sixteenth at Augusta was a lovely short par 3 that ranged from 100 to 150 yards in length. Two tees were provided and used alternately depending on the hole location. Mike Miller has painted the hole here in the initial stages when the pine forests were still thin, casting just enough shadow to add even more beauty to this already lovely setting.*

MacKenzie and Jones stated repeatedly that Augusta was not a theme course composed of replica holes, but instead, that much of its architecture was inspired by certain concepts the two had seen elsewhere. MacKenzie wrote:

"It has been suggested that it was our intention at Augusta to produce copies of the most famous golf holes. Any attempt of this kind could only result in failure. It may be possible to reproduce a famous picture, but the charm of a golf hole may be dependent on a background of sand dunes, trees, or even mountains several miles away. A copy without the surroundings might create an unnatural appearance and cause a feeling of irritation, instead of charm. On the other hand, it is well to have a mental picture of the world's outstanding holes and to use this knowledge in reproducing their finest golfing features, and perhaps even improving on them. At Augusta we tried to produce eighteen ideal holes, not copies of classical holes but embodying their best features, with other features suggested by the nature of the terrain. We hope for accomplishments of such unique character that the holes will be looked upon as classics in themselves."

Augusta National's Sixteenth, circa 1932

36 x 48, oil on panel, 2000 | Course: Augusta National Golf Club, Augusta, Georgia | Architects: Alister MacKenzie and Bobby Jones

Third at Fox Hills, Dusk, circa 1933

36 x 48, oil on panel, 1998 | Course: Fox Hills Golf Course, Baldwin Hills, California (no longer exists) | Architects: George C. Thomas Jr. and Billy Bell

THIRD AT FOX HILLS, DUSK, CIRCA 1933: *One of Mike Miller's most complex images, this par 4 of 400 yards at the former 36-hole public facility created by Thomas and Bell proves that artistic bunkering can be built on public courses just as easily as it can on private layouts. There is a peculiar mentality in modern day golf that certain artistic touches and looks can't be introduced on municipal courses, and that hazards must be "dumbed-down" for public golf. The resulting lack of interesting architecture found in American public golf might explain the disturbing figures that show that the same numbers of people who take up the game each year are matched by the number who quit playing. Imagine if museums or musical events were only available to people of certain social status or clubs? The spirit of our country would certainly not be what it is, yet the situation in golf is one of two very distinct groups: that which is exposed to artistry in design, and that which isn't.*

Golf architecture does not need to be vastly different for public and private golf. Architects will claim cost is a factor for not creating better designs, or more commonly, that the need to improve speed of play dictates their lack of thought-provoking and interesting design injected into public design. However, as Thomas and Bell proved at this now lost facility, a balance between interest and playability could be created. Thomas was a believer in public golf dictating the future of the game in America, and he even spent his own money to finish construction of the 36-hole courses at Griffith Park in Los Angeles. Thomas once wrote:

"It is most important for the future of golf in this country that every aid should be given to the building and upkeep of municipal courses, because such will eventually become of the greatest value to the game, and from them we may expect to produce many of our future great players."

TIMBER POINT'S TWELFTH, CIRCA 1925: *Painstakingly constructed over two years, Timber Point Golf Club was C.H. Alison's American masterpiece. Situated on Long Island's Great South Bay, 100 acres of the original site was marshland that Alison reclaimed and filled with beach sand. The front nine traveled through a dense forest, with enormous bunkers protecting the fairways and greens. The eighth and ninth holes emerged from the trees and played through sand and marshland before returning to the clubhouse. The entire back nine was played on the Point, with the highlights being the 140-yard par-3 twelfth (depicted here) and the 200-yard par-3 fifteenth.*

Timber Point struggled through the Great Depression and World War II and was eventually sold to Suffolk County, which turned it into a 27-hole facility in 1972 with little remaining today of the Colt and Alison design. Timber Point may be the most depressing example of fine architecture no longer available for public consumption, and to the detriment of the art of golf architecture.

Timber Point's Twelfth, circa 1925

36 x 48, oil on panel, 1999 | Course: Timber Point Golf Club, Great South Bay, New York | Architect: C.H. Alison

Good visibility is indispensable if the holes are to present a problem which needs to be thought out with thoroughness in the matter of attack. But visibility should not be unduly stressed, and blindness of a kind can be a virtue.

TOM SIMPSON, GOLF ARCHITECT

To Frame or Not to Frame?

During the last part of the twentieth century golf course designers placed great emphasis on the "framing" of holes, with little architectural focus on the creation of thought-provoking, strategic situations. Backdrops, cart path camouflage, tree plantings, and bowled fairways telling the golfer how to play became the architect's top priority at the expense of spirited, challenging, and mentally-stimulating holes.

In other words, golf architecture became shallow.

Although many "pretty" landscapes have been created in recent times, few have had much playing appeal after the first or second go-around. It's the result of an overreliance on petty, unnatural thrills and a lack of genuine playing excitement.

Much of the blame for this "framing" style of design does not fall on the shoulders of architects. Instead, the culpability starts with powerful golf magazine ranking panels who have placed an equal or even greater emphasis on elements such as aesthetics, resistance to scoring, conditioning, and country club ambiance as they have on the variety of strategic and original design qualities. The architects, claiming the "need" to put food on the table as they charge upward of a million dollars for a design, are anxious to earn awards and see their courses ranked. So at the expense of the art, they have merely followed the rankings' lead and given the panelists what they like to see in their limited trips around America's latest and greatest courses.

This is not to downplay the importance of the "experience" in golf, but instead to put its role in perspective. No one can discount that the little nuances of a facility and service-related aspects genuinely add to the fun of going to certain places in golf. However, equally weighing the quality of the food, the beauty of the entrance drive, and the density of the men's grill milkshakes has taken the attention away from sound architecture and time devoted by architects or developers to creating interesting playing situations. It's akin to seeing a movie and judging the merits of the film by the ticket taker's friendliness, the taste of the popcorn, the previews shown, and the comfort of your seat. Those are all elements that add to your movie-going experience, but they should not influence your analysis of the film and the manner in which the story entertains, engages or enlightens you.

As we know from studying the most lasting golf designs, the "experience" can only mask architectural flaws for so long. The great courses rarely hold the player's hand. They offer plenty of surprises and nuances that take as many as 100 rounds to grasp. Sure, the master architects often created aesthetic wonders that also happened to be beautifully framed with nice "experiences," but mostly they injected other attributes into the golf holes themselves that made their work interesting to experience repeatedly.

There is no denying that beauty is an integral component of great golf holes. Whenever possible, lovely situations should be taken advantage of and emphasized for effect. However, the playing interest and character of holes should never become a secondary priority to aesthetics. Great golf holes can be both beautiful and interesting to play over and over again.

It's no different than the decline in the art of filmmaking. Hollywood has shifted its emphasis from story to visual effects, and few can say with a straight face that there is much lasting quality to a majority of Tinseltown's recent output. The films that endure and give us the most emotional satisfaction are those with a great story at their core. Sure, they are also wonderful to look at thanks to skillful cinematography, special effects, or deft editing, but in the end it is the director's ability to convey a compelling story that matters most. Then the filmmakers must complement that story with strong acting, an appropriate musical score, and the proper presentation to make the film even stronger. Many elements are involved, but the story still holds the film together and drives the audience's desire to watch it closely.

The same goes for golf architecture. The soul of design is not in the definition or the framing of the hole, but in the architect's ability to present fascinating strategy (his story). The golf architect accents his script by taking advantage of natural contours, creating artistic bunkers, and adding subtle aesthetic touches (his special effects).

The recent trend in golf has been to focus on the surrounds and backdrops of holes. Millions are spent to place the emphasis on defining how the hole is played and making every single feature perfectly visible to the golfer so that a pretty, "fair" design is created. This may sound like a noble cause in the name of fairness, but the problem is no different than other attempts to please too many. It comes at the expense of the occasional thought-provoking visual impairment or the chance to find a new angle of attack to a hole. Holding the player's hand by making everything visible strips substance from a course and eventually kills any ability to inspire the golfer. Without a compelling "story," a design eventually becomes dull no matter how beautiful it is to look at.

One prominent modern designer who has designed many courses "well-received in the marketplace" (his words, not mine), has made a killing by moving vast amounts of earth and stocking the sides of his holes with trees and useless bunkers in order to "frame" every shot. In essence, he creates a comfortably pleasing landscape design, not golf architecture. His ultraexpensive courses make a big splash in the rankings and in all but a few cases fall just as fast off the dreaded lists within five to ten years. Which tells us that even the most architecturally-challenged ranking panelists are initially attracted to his work because of its beauty, but ultimately tire of his courses because there is nothing to think about nor any compelling reason to return for a second or third time around.

This architect's success in "defining" holes and his obsession with their "framing" is a peculiar notion for any art form, but particularly when you apply the concept to Mike Miller's landscapes. The notion that framing is what genuinely gives the golf hole its structure (not the strategy), is no different than saying Miller's landscapes are lacking charm until they are put into the right frames. And if the frame selected by the frame store personnel doesn't work, somehow the image Miller has created cannot stand on its own and must be reframed to attempt to recapture some semblance of order and beauty.

Do Miller's images genuinely rely on frames for their character, depth, color, and overall attractiveness? If so, wouldn't we have included reproductions of the images here in their frames?

Does music rely on its packaging and liner notes for the ultimate listening satisfaction? Does another three-dimensional art form such as sculpture, need framing to accent the art?

To further delve into this question of framing holes and the notion of creating a perfect visual definition, consider the three finest holes in golf and determine if their framing is the primary component leading to their timeless character, or is it their strategy?

Is the par-3 sixteenth at Cypress Point special because of its dramatic shot over the Pacific Ocean? Absolutely. It would be foolish to contend that the beauty and the "framing" here is not a wonderful attribute of this hole and would not make this a special hole regardless of the MacKenzie design. However, over time there is little question that the sixteenth has endured because of its tempting qualities. It is special to play by virtue of the decision that the golfer must make every time they tee it up. The golfer must ask, "Do I go for the green?" or "Do I layup well left and take a chance with a wedge shot and a putt?" Or, "Do I lay-up as close to the green as possible, take a little more risk but increase my chances to make a par?"

When all is said and done, the tempting decisions that come into play on Cypress Point's sixteenth hole make this and other long par 3s with similar resolve so satisfying to play. Replace the Pacific Ocean with an abandoned quarry (the modern rage) and the hole may not be the most photographed in golf, but it'll still be a hole of genuine merit and nearly equal satisfaction to play because of the tempting choices offered.

What about the thirteenth hole at Augusta National, a course that has undergone a "reframing" because its "frame didn't fit" (again, the remodeler's words, not mine). Sure, the flowering azaleas, the shadows created by the towering pines and the lovely little creek fronting the green all conspire to make this par 5 one of golf's most beautifully framed holes. But do we enjoy watching the best players in the world tackle it because it is pleasing to watch their ball travel against the framing pines? Do the azaleas affect the fascinating decision-making that goes on here?

Again, the heart and soul of this brilliant hole is in its tempting qualities and the difficulty of the shots required. The temptation is derived from the fascinating contour of the ground, the relatively short yardage, the angle of the green, the sharp bend of the hole, the location of the hazard, and the thirteenth's situation in the round. Take away the flowering azaleas, the chemically-induced greenery, the tall pines, and the blue-dyed water, and you still have one of the best holes in golf because of the inherent strategy created by its architects, Alister MacKenzie and Bobby Jones.

Finally, the most interesting example of all is the seventeenth, or the Road Hole at St. Andrews. It has to be one of the worst-framed, most poorly defined tee shots in golf. It is not attractive, the landing area blinded, and yet your options become fairly well understood after one time around. The challenge and excitement it evokes never goes away thanks to the manner in which the green sits up in beguiling fashion, teasing the player to make up their mind about whether to play it safe or not. Nothing about the Road Hole is well-framed or pleasant except for its consistent ability to excite the senses and repeatedly rattle the golfer's nerves. The lack of framing does not hinder the hole in any way, but in fact, lends to its charm and originality because there is much to be discovered here during multiple rounds.

Is the framing mentality in modern architecture a fad or is it here to stay? After all, golfers love well-framed holes and you can't go more than a week or so without hearing a Tour player cite a course's greatness because "everything is right in front of you." But Tour players naturally want their hands held and the holes they play to offer no surprises, no bad lies, and no chance of unfair incidents occurring. They are trying to make a living on these layouts and naturally don't want to have anything out of their control. And, sadly, modern golf is caving in to their demand at the expense of the sporting spirit of golf.

After all, baseball hitters would love to know the type of spin each pitch will have, where it will cross home plate, and what speed it'll be coming at. However, if the players and managers knew what the pitcher was going to spring on them, baseball would lose much of its charm. It could become a mere contest between throwing and slugging robots who don't think or feel anything (which I'm sure the owners would love; the robots would work a lot cheaper).

But in golf, why can't we have the best of both worlds? Subtly-framed, attractive holes that quench everyone's thirst for beauty, combined with mentally stimulating options and interesting battles against natural elements that tempt us to pull off shots we never would have imagined trying, and which ultimately reward the better player?

The elaborate combination of beauty and strategy requires architects to spend time working out the strategy of each hole and making adjustments in the field as construction progresses. Putting these holes on paper is one thing, but actually making them work once the ground has been cleared is another story.

The ability to build visually stunning holes while also making players think is what separates the work of Pete Dye from many other architects in recent years. Dye has proved you can furnish the best of both worlds. He understands that dramatic looking holes will draw golfers in to see what all the fuss is about, but also knows that a few semiblind shots, some quirky contours, optional routes of play, and deep bunkers will get the players contemplating the possibilities. And as Dye has been known to say about Tour players, "When you get those dudes thinking, they're in trouble."

The real answer to moving beyond the mysteriously shallow framing mentality lies with the architects. Let's face it, when one of the most successful architects in golf is called in to make a tournament course more challenging and he admits that "defining holes" might help the golfer "line up some," there is some confusion here by the people who should understand the basics of golf architecture. You have someone brought in to make pars more dearly bought and to keep scores and the players in check (a practice that in itself is rather pathetic), yet he is in essence stripping the thinking element from what was once considered the greatest man-made strategic course in the world, Augusta National. And ultimately, defining the holes and narrowing the corridors makes a course simpler and less of a mental challenge for the top players in the world, and a far less entertaining layout for spectators.

The most frightening consequence of the modern day framing mentality is the potential for what these architects would do if given the opportunity to tinker with the wide, undefined, and quirky British Isles links courses. Would they import trees and stick them on top of dunes in relatively straight lines in order to frame the holes and narrow them down? Would they plant a swarm of azaleas around the Swilken Bridge at St. Andrews to hide it? Maybe place a couple of clover shaped bunkers in front of the home hole green on the Old Course to define the hole locations better since the green is only protected today by a severe undulation and out-of-bounds to the right and rear?

It is hard to believe such radical and embarrassing changes could occur, but who would have ever thought they'd have rough and moveable pines at Augusta in direct opposition to Bobby Jones's vision for his dream course?

The truth is, all golfers prefer to have infrequent surprises because there is less chance we will get into trouble or have our score blemished by a big number. We like to have everything in front of us so that we don't have to think. But after all is said and done, this kind of golf bores us because the courses that genuinely excite us over time throw some curves. Consciously or not, golfers learn to understand this and relish these challenges. If they hadn't, there are some pretty famous holes and courses featured in this book that would not be around today.

The golfer needs surprises and some uncertainty in their architecture to keep their golf fresh. They want to be tempted to try a shot where there is some unforeseen trouble that they suspect is there but which they aren't quite sure about. Golf architects need to focus on creating more strategic design and put a little less time into framing for the long-term good of the sport.

Because as George Thomas once wrote, the strategy is the soul of the game. Ultimately, the framing mentality in golf will fail to appeal because it lacks soul.

Blindness

BY MAX BEHR, 1926

As to visibility, Mr. A.C.M. Croone gave the British view when he remarked in the London *Field* that "St. Andrews suffers no loss because the approach shot to round a dozen of the putting greens is in greater or less degree blind." By this is not meant that they are in greater or less degree blind from all angles. It simply means that, according to the British view, blindness is on occasions a legitimate and delightful hazard, and especially so when it forces the player to make a placement shot to attain visibility.

But blindness in an undulating, tumbling terrain such as that which links land presents is quite different from what we are subject to in this country. The greens are not separate creations apart from the whole. They are as the Creator made them. They belong. The eye can pick up distance as it wanders from one hillock to the next till it arrives at the pin. It does not meet with a sudden blockage such as an artificially created green, the contours of which are separate and apart from its surroundings. Such is the character of blindness at St. Andrews.

Blindness is certainly a subject in golf that one can go blind arguing about. There would seem to be no justification for it. And yet I would like to make an observation which may possibly explain the pleasure it excites with some. It is certainly true that as players of games we endeavor to prolong the time when we must show our hand. We try to blind our opponent to our intent. This imposes upon him the task of anticipating our hidden purpose. Thus there is occasioned a sparring of wits aside from the mere skill required to play games. Blindness, therefore, makes a call upon intelligence. It comes down to the question as to whether the character of the deception is legitimate. The pitcher in baseball cannot make a fake pass to throw a player out at first base. That is not playing ball. Therefore if blindness be such that we are continually deceived, it is only natural that we should object to it. But if the deception is such that we can with intelligence overcome it, then it must certainly be accounted an asset.

Blindness is the one type of hazard in golf which contains the element of mystery. If we were not all so concerned with our scores, and, instead played golf for the pleasure in playing the strokes, blindness would not be so abhorrent to us as it is today. At St. Andrews it is perhaps the peculiar blending of blindness with visibility that has intrigued one great golfer after another to pronounce it *the* great course. Mere skill in stroking the ball is not sufficient to solve its problems. One can play upon it year after year and never wholly fathom its secrets.

Naturalness in Golf Architecture

BY MAX BEHR, 1926

The Nature the golf architect has in mind is one associated with golf, and this is linksland upon which golf has been played for hundreds of years, and remained through a major part of this time uncontaminated by the hand of man except for the cutting of the holes. Whatever beauty such land possessed was inherent in it, and those today who have played golf amidst such primeval surroundings are conscious of a certain charm wholly lacking upon a palpable man-made golf course.

In this country architects are presented with few locations the topography of which is ideally fitted for the playing of golf. Hence, the architect must improve upon Nature. But such improvements have primarily to with rendering Nature suitable for golf, and do not necessarily involve any improvement of Nature itself except for the definite purpose in hand.

Is it important that the architect should endeavor to go further and combine art with the utilitarian side of his work? It would seem so. And for this reason: Golf courses constructed with the limited idea of merely creating a playground around which one may bat a ball comfortably make possible only the efforts of one side of the contest, that of the golfer, and owing to this neglect, he finds himself confronted with a landscape brutalized with the ideas of some other golfer. Does he object?

Of course he does. He too has ideas of his own. Consequently the history of every artificial appearing golf course is one of continual change. There is a very practical lesson in this and one that can be translated into dollars and cents. And this is that golf architecture can only be rendered permanent by art. Art is usually associated in the mind with the aesthetic, but if we comprehend it in a larger sense, it will be seen that only by art is every walk of life rendered stable and enduring. If, then, for practical reasons we are justified in looking upon golf architecture as an art and not merely a means to an end, we shall find it closely akin to landscape gardening. What are the requisites to perfection in this art? Humphrey Repton, the great landscape gardener of the XVIII Century, has perhaps most concisely and perfectly stated them:

"First it must display the natural beauties and hide the natural defects of every situation. Secondly, it should give the appearance of any extent and freedom by carefully disguising or hiding the boundary. Thirdly, it must studiously conceal every interference of art, however expensive, by which the scenery is improved making the whole appear the production of nature only; and, fourthly, all objects of mere convenience or comfort, if incapable of being made ornamental, or of becoming proper parts of the general scenery, must be removed or concealed."

It may never be possible to live up to such an ideal in golf architecture. In endeavoring to create an harmonious whole there are bunkers, greens, fairways and rough to be considered. Nevertheless where it is necessary to modify the ground to create these features, their contours can be made to seem as if they had always been, and their civilized aspect, because necessary to golf, will not be an affront to the natural beauty they reveal.

FOURTEENTH AT CRYSTAL DOWNS: *The attractive 140-yard par-3 fourteenth at Crystal Downs sits beautifully among trees, bunkers, and rustic areas with the shoreline of Lake Michigan and the Sleeping Bear Dunes in the distance. No doubt this is one of the most beautiful holes on a course full of dramatic surprises at seemingly every tee. Ultimately though, the genuine beauty of this hole lies in the fascinating green complex and the many different shots required to negotiate this one-shotter. It follows one of the most difficult par 4s in golf, so the short iron shot here is a welcome respite. However, the front portion of the green is steeply sloped, making downhill putts to the front hole locations very difficult. The rear hole locations, particularly left, are the most challenging because no golfer ever gets completely comfortable playing bold shots here due to the steep drop-off to the rear of the green. The lack of framing directly behind the green also adds to the dilemmas here for the golfer. If trees framed the rear of the green, judging distances and determining the effect of wind would be rather simple. But because the rear is open, more issues are placed before the golfer to deal with, making a relatively short shot that much more interesting. The fourteenth tee is out of view and slightly to the right of this angle. The hole is pictured in a late 1990s rendition, with the bunkers perhaps a bit more regular in shape and certainly more evolved than in MacKenzie and Maxwell's original design.*

MacKenzie's and Maxwell's fourteenth at Crystal Downs seems to qualify under MacKenzie's definition of an ideal hole: "There are few problems more difficult to solve than the problem of what actually constitutes an ideal links or an ideal hole, but it is comparatively safe to say that the ideal hole is one that affords the greatest pleasure to the greatest number, gives the fullest advantage for accurate play, stimulates players to improve their game, and which never becomes monotonous."

Fourteenth at Crystal Downs, circa 1997

36 x 48, oil on panel (1998) | Course: Crystal Downs Country Club, Frankfort, Michigan | Architects: Alister MacKenzie and Perry Maxwell

Storm Breaking Up, Thirteenth at Pine Valley, circa 1935

36 x 48, oil on panel, 2000 | Course: Pine Valley Golf Club, Pine Valley, New Jersey | Architect: George Crump

STORM BREAKING UP, THIRTEENTH AT PINE VALLEY, CIRCA 1935: *Many consider this 446-yard par 4 to be the finest in golf, and few can name an existing hole that is a finer combination of art, strategy and challenge. Besides its beauty and flair for the dramatic, the thirteenth at Pine Valley tempts and challenges like few others. It also, incidentally, does all of this without relying on its framing. In fact, an argument can be made that the evolution of "framing" around this green, particularly to the left in the form of tall pines, takes some of the drama away from this hole.*

Trees have encroached much closer to the green today than in this early 1930s view by Mike Miller. Here we also see the course in its early years with more sand than shrubbery in the hazards, and with shorter trees. (As of 1925, no pines were even planted as saplings in the area left of the green. This suggests Crump and others preferred the "exposed" nature of the thirteenth green complex.)

Though the hole plays similarly today in terms of sheer difficulty, it could be argued that the thirteenth was more mentally taxing in the early days due to less "framing." With the element of wind in play due to the absence of trees and with distances harder to gauge because of a lack of framing, the player is forced to take in more information. And visually, the more exposed the green appears, the more intimidating a target it becomes. And only when presented with a great deal of information do we really find out who the best players are.

Either way, when looking at Miller's portrayal here, Robert Hunter's remark about Pine Valley comes to mind: "These superb hazards are a part of nature. Where does art begin?"

APPROACH TO THE SIXTH, CYPRESS POINT, CIRCA 1928: *The 516-yard, par-5 sixth at Cypress Point is one of the most beautifully framed green sites in golf, complete with attractive bunkering, towering Monterey pines and natural dunes. But it is also one of the most interesting strategic par 5s in golf and derives much of its lasting pleasure from the difficulties presented by MacKenzie and Hunter. Some might even call the strategy here bizarre or unorthodox. As a dogleg left hole, most would assume the closer the tee shot is played to the inside of the dogleg, the shorter the hole becomes. However, the steep slope of the fairway actually rewards a right-to-left tee shot that starts down the far right side of the fairway and utilizes the slope to gain yardage. From there the player has a good chance to go at this green in two shots.*

The bunkers short and left of the green are the main concern on the approach; that is, if your eye is not too caught up in the stunning rear bunker. However, it's the approach to this green that is the most attractive because the architects kept the right-hand side open. Missing the green to the right leaves a difficult recovery and many players have wished they had laid up short of the green where the up-and-down is simpler.

Robert Hunter had this to say about the design of approaches to greens, another dying art in the modern day emphasis on target golf. Hunter wrote in The Links, *"...let us turn our thoughts for one moment to the entrance to the green. There is no portion of a golf course which requires more care at the time of construction, and more attention later in the upkeep, than the area upon which most approaches to the hole will land. What decisive and subtle influences may be made to work upon the ball at just this point!"*

Approach to the Sixth, Cypress Point, circa 1928

36 x 48, oil on panel, 1999 | Course: Cypress Point Club, Pebble Beach, California | Architects: Alister MacKenzie and Robert Hunter

Rocky Cove and Fifteenth Green, Cypress Point, circa 1930

36 x 48, oil on panel, 1998 | Course: Cypress Point Club, Pebble Beach, California | Architects: Alister MacKenzie and Robert Hunter

ROCKY COVE AND FIFTEENTH GREEN, CYPRESS POINT, CIRCA 1930: *The sixteenth hole is always the most anticipated adventure at Cypress Point, but the preceding fifteenth is certainly more fun for players of all skill levels because it's within reach at only 140 yards. Perhaps the most beautiful setting in golf, who can argue that this hole does not derive much of its excellence from its setting?*

But MacKenzie expressed concern and considered it less than ideal because little strategy was injected into this remarkable green complex. Thus, he created a right-side cup location near where Mike Miller has placed the flagstick in this reproduction. MacKenzie included this location as the more tempting option in competitive play to lend a risk-and-reward characteristic to the hole. But still, he was never fully satisfied with the nature of this hole relying on beauty more than all else for its popularity. Or at least, that's the view he put in print:

"It is not by any means ideal, as there are not a sufficient number of alternative shots necessary to play it. It is at its best when the flag is placed on the little tongue of green that projects between the bunkers on the right. In this position one has the alternative of playing an extremely difficult pitch with the chance of a two, or playing safe to the center of the green and being content with a three. The hole owes its reputation almost entirely to the beauty of the green and its surroundings."

SUNRISE AT SAND HILLS, SEVENTH HOLE : *On a course full of beautiful holes, none stands out more for its tempting strategic quality than the 283-yard par-4 seventh. The fairway is wide and it is to the right of the area shown here by Mike Miller. Rear cup locations cannot be seen in this view, but can be seen from certain locations in the fairway if the player places his tee shot properly. Yet place your tee ball too safely, and the banked fairway leaves you a shot with a distorted view of the green.*

Simple strategy, and yet it takes many rounds to understand the nuances of this hole. The one constant is the gaping bunker detailed here by Mike Miller. The words of C.B. Macdonald, who Coore and Crenshaw admire as much as any architect they've studied, seem most appropriate in looking at this painting. They are also still the most vital in considering the state of golf architecture as an art form. Macdonald wrote:

"A golf hole, humanly speaking, is like life, inasmuch as one cannot judge justly of any person's character the first time one meets him. Sometimes it takes years to discover and appreciate hidden qualities which only time discloses, and he usually discloses them on the links. No real lover of golf with artistic understanding would undertake to measure the quality or fascination of a golf hole by a yard-stick, any more than a critic of poetry would attempt to measure the supreme sentiment expressed in a poem by the same method. One can understand the meter, but one cannot measure the soul expressed. It is absolutely inconceivable."

Sunrise at Sand Hills, Seventh Hole

22 x 28, oil on panel, 1999 | Course: Sand Hills Golf Club, Mullen, Nebraska | Architects: Bill Coore and Ben Crenshaw

*I believe in reverencing anything in the life of man which
has the testimony of the ages as being unexcelled, whether
it be literature, paintings, poetry, tombs – even a golf hole.*

C.B. MACDONALD

Afterword

If in some way the genuine beauty of art in golf architecture is more apparent to you now, then we have accomplished our goal. Unfortunately, when critical suggestions are passed around as they have been in this book, one can never offer enough "solutions" to the problems addressed here without sounding particularly pessimistic.

But the "art" of golf architecture is at such an odd crossroads that strong words and images are necessary. Frank discussion is a necessity if this art is to grow.

Ironically, architecture today faces dilemmas that were confronted in the early 1920s and the art has since regressed to the point it is in serious jeopardy of disintegrating altogether. The transformations in the field of architecture are those that need the most urgent attention; namely, the freedom to constructively criticize or even discuss architecture without repercussion, along with the need for hands-on involvement by the architect in the day-to-day planning and building of his design.

Two "anonymous" articles from the USGA Green Section Bulletin provide a glimpse of these emerging issues from 80 years ago, and furnish an appropriate ending for this text. Both essays make a strong case for a safe return of the aforementioned issues in contemporary architecture, just as they did nearly 80 years ago. One possible author of these "anonymous" essays was Max Behr, although they may have been written by Alan and Hugh Wilson, prominent contributors to the Bulletin who would have preferred writing these brief essays anonymously because of their stature in the game as "amateur" architects. Then again, the essays could have been written by some wise man who was simply in too powerful a position to incur the wrath of his peers for crafting such honest, eloquent words. Whatever the case, the author addresses the need for criticism in golf architecture and the avenue to progress for the future of this art form.

In closing, let me wish you good luck in your golfing endeavors, and offer my thanks for devoting your time to the wonderful art form known as golf architecture.

The Need for Criticism in Golf Architecture

ANONYMOUS, 1923

There is a positive if indefinable relation between the character of a golf course and the pleasure derived by the golfer. The character or degree of excellence of a course depends on three things: First, its architecture; second, its standard of maintenance; and third, its landscape beauty. In the betterment of any golf course, all three of these elements are essential, and the excellence of golf courses will improve in proportion as golfers realize their importance. It is true that golfers get a lot of fun out of a simple course laid out in an old pasture; but it does not follow that such a course is to be considered a model.

There was a time when the professional golfer was supposed to be a Pooh Bah who knew all about playing the game, everything about greenkeeping, and the whole subject of golf architecture. Today nearly everyone recognizes these three things as distinct though interrelated subjects, and justly distrusts the man who claims to be proficient in all three or even in two of them. In other words, specialization has entered golf as in other fields where progress is usually in proportion to intensive studies of limited scope. The day of the man who assumed expertness in all phases of golf has gone the way of the Ichthyosaurs.

In the evolution of any particular subject, frank discussion of principles and methods helps to promote advancement. There certainly has been and still is abundant discussion as to playing the game of golf, and usually with the assumption that the form of the latest champion is the best. Every one has perfect freedom to present his experience and theories on how to grow grass. When it comes to golf architecture, however, there is practically nothing in print, but by word of mouth one often hears violent expressions of opinion in which the word "rotten" is frequently used. The relative immunity of golf architecture to critical discussion is partly due to the fact that it involves the architect himself, or in other words is likely to be taken as personal criticism. There is likewise a vague sort of unwritten law akin to lese majesty which to a great extent absolves artists (including architects) from criticism. Finally the architects themselves maintain a sort of guild—they do not publicly discuss or criticize each other's ideas, nor do they write books or articles for the education of the golfing world. This condition of affairs is not a healthful one for the progress of golf architecture.

In spite of these strictures there has been progress in golf architecture, mostly by a very few men. It is depressing to see many new courses built in which the construction features deserve only censure. In the effort to construct something novel, the result is often one that excites only ridicule. Incidentally such caricatures reveal that the architect is only human—not, as we were fain to believe, one of Nietsche's supermen. And so the architect must submit to criticism like any other mortal.

One of the notable advances in golf architecture in America was made when the National Links were built by Mr. Charles B. Macdonald, each hole being a more or less exact replica of one in Europe which had become well known. Valuable as this plan may be, there are two obvious limitations. First of all, if used generally there could be no progress but merely constant replications of the holes chosen as best. Second, there is wide divergence of opinion in regard to certain well-known holes, some architects insisting they are in reality not famous for their good qualities but infamous for their bad traits. Clearly a discussion by the different architects over the merits or demerits of particular holes could not help but be educational. But the architects remain silent, and it is becoming increasingly apparent that the discussions will have to be by the growing number of amateurs who are making a study of golf architecture. Such amateurs are not content either with the explanation that a hole is a replica of one that is noted, or with the architect's ex cathedra pronouncement that the hole is superb. The amateur student of architecture asks himself such questions as these: Is the green properly placed? Is it of the best size and shape and properly undulated? Are the bunkers correctly placed and of the right size to be fair? Etc. In the answer to such questions neither authority nor tradition should have influence. The attitude must be that of the scientist, who remains skeptical until the proof is sufficient.

As an outcome of this growing amateur interest in golf architecture, it is not surprising to find work of very superior character being done by non-professional architects. Indeed, it is not too much to say that such amateurs are outstripping the professional architects in the excellence of their work. This is doubtless due in part to the fact that such amateurs devote far more time and study to the building of a particular hole than does the professional architect. If this be the true explanation, then many architects are endangering their reputations by undertaking too much work—which naturally leads to a sort of made-in-the-factory type of architecture.

The golf clubs are vitally interested in this matter because golf courses are expensive and the members like to have a course that excites admiration, not one that calls for adverse criticism. The architects owe it to the clubs, from which they derive their support, and also to themselves, to aid in getting better architecture and in suppressing freak construction. It is earnestly urged that they abandon the policy of secretiveness and silence and discuss frankly the good and bad architectural features of golf courses—to the end that golf progress be furthered.

The Progress of Golf Architecture

ANONYMOUS, 1925

Golf architecture involves far more than the laying out of a definite number of holes each of a virtually standardized length. That these lengths are standardized can hardly be questioned, even if the distances are only approximately equal and those decreed by what golfers think best. There is general agreement that the desirable total length of eighteen holes should be between 6,000 and 6,500 yards. If one should judge from a large proportion of golf courses, the designer had no other end in view than that stated above, namely a course whose measurements approximate a standard. There is seldom any indication of originality, except of the freaky kind, and rarely any conception of landscape beauty. Apart from the relatively mathematical or mechanical features of golf course building, which any-one can learn quickly, there lies the whole art, which will make or break the reputation of every golf architect. Only the sluggish mind of an easily satisfied public has blinded it to the hideousness of most of our golf courses. Sometimes the beauty of the surroundings helps to con-ceal the ugliness of the artificial work, though the lack of any harmony be only too obvious. Fortunately, perhaps, many architects make their artificial work concealed or half-concealed, such as blind bunkers. Otherwise its unloveliness would be too patent.

This may sound like the writing of one suffering a severe attack of indigestion. It is meant to be the expres-sion of feeling of one who is saddened by the absence of landscape beauty in too much of the artificial construc-tions on golf courses. A sand bunker can be made a thing of beauty or a hideous gash. Fortunately many of the latter are built "blind." The artificial lines can be curves that fit in with those of the terrain, or they can be angular and jar every sense of harmony. After all, a golf architect worthy of the name must be an artist, painting his ideas on the face of Nature as his canvas. The painter retouches his work again and again. Too many architects make the mechanical plans and leave practically all else to the construction gang. Some indeed work on a cut-and-dried series of mod-els, which are reproduced here, there and yonder regardless of the terrain. When you see one course built by such an architect, you can recognize at once every other course he has built. This is true not in the sense that one can learn to recognize a Corot or a Landsdowne, but true to actual mechanical details. There is merit in the idea that holes of proven reputation ought to be copied—especially if these replicas apply as to principles but not as to details. If however this idea is embalmed in a set of mechanical models, then there can obviously be no progress as long as these are followed, neither for the architect himself nor for his art. To be blunt, such an architect is sacrificing his art to present commercial gain.

Perhaps the architect is not so much to blame as is the golfing public. As long as there is no criticism, he may well believe that he is producing meritorious results. A few courses built in recent years are examples of splendid land-scape architecture. The influence of these will doubtless stimulate golfers to demand better work from the archi-tects. To build artistic curves will require more of the architect's time than he takes at present. It can not be done, especially in its finishing stages, by a brief visit once a month or so. That is too much like a landscape artist hiring a journeyman painter to paint pictures for him. It can be done, of course, but the results are not inspiring.

Golf architects ought to be leaders in promoting progress of golf. They are not. Today many courses are being built by professional golf players that are as good as or better than those made by most professional architects. Except for a few notable exceptions in the profession, the term architect can hardly be used at present as relating to golf architects. There are also a goodly number of amateurs who have done very beautiful work which can truly be called artistic. Every architect owes it both to himself and to the golfing world to strive toward perfection. We believe it will be more profitable to him to build fewer and better courses.

There is progress for the betterment of golf architecture, but it is very slow. It will continue to be slow as long as the artistic sense is sacrificed to immediate commercial gain.

Acknowledgments

MICHAEL G. MILLER

My deep felt gratitude to essayist Geoff Shackelford for his expertise and assistance in the technical aspects of the golf architecture depicted in this volume. An exceptional thank you and special recognition to Mr. Gene Mako, under whose decade of training I was given a comprehension of the principles of fine art. Additionally, my heartfelt gratitude to James and Bernice McCombie, Sorrell and Linda Trope, Al and Shirley Scheid, Jerry Crumpler, Ran Morrissett, Paul Latshaw and Gil Hanse whose patronage has allowed me to continue in my chosen career. Also thank you to Taba Dale of Scottsdale Collection, Inc. for her confidence and faith, to golf professional Ed Coleman for his interest and knowledge, and to Jerry Soloman for his kind support. And lastly, the most important thank you to my parents, Dr. David and Mrs. Ann Miller and family, for their collective unflagging support and encouragement.

GEOFF SHACKELFORD

Special thanks to all of those who have encouraged me to seek out true art in golf architecture. Especially to Mike Miller for creating images that give all of us a new outlook on golf architecture and a fresh look at many classic courses from the past. I must also express my gratitude to Gil Hanse, both for reading the early draft of this text and for allowing me to assist him on a design project. The numerous days walking "in the field" with various members of the community and on my own time has given me a new outlook on golf architecture which added immeasurably to my perspective while writing these essays. And of course none of the contributions in this book from past architects would have been possible without the help of Saundra Sheffer and Marge Dewey of the currently inactive Ralph W. Miller Golf Library. Hopefully this wonderful collection will have a new home by the time this book is in your hands. Finally, thank you to all of those who discuss the art of golf architecture with such passion.

About the Contributors

Michael G. Miller was the Director of Golf at Riviera Country Club from 1993-98 and a golf professional for 28 years. He began painting in 1985 and has been creating golf landscapes since 1996. He currently resides in Los Angeles.

Geoff Shackelford's previous books on golf include *The Riviera Country Club...A Definitive History*, *The Captain, Masters of the Links, The Good Doctor Returns, The Golden Age of Golf Design*, and *Alister MacKenzie's Cypress Point Club*. He resides in Santa Monica, California and can be reached at geoffshackelford@aol.com.

Max Behr was the first editor of *Golf Illustrated* and wrote extensively on golf throughout his life after a fine amateur golfing career. In the early 1920s he designed Lakeside Golf Club, Rancho Santa Fe Country Club and several other fine courses, all in California.

Robert Hunter supervised construction of Cypress Point and The Valley Club of Montecito for Alister MacKenzie. He authored *The Links* (1926) and wrote many articles on golf.

Harry S. Colt was one of golf's first professional architects and creator of noted courses such as Sunningdale and St. George's Hill. He co-wrote Some Essays on Golf Architecture with C.H. Alison.

Bernard Darwin was the most prolific writer in the history of golf and probably the finest. He was one of the first early twentieth-century figures to write about golf architecture.

Tom Simpson and H.N. Wethered authored *The Architectural Side of Golf* (1929). Mr. Simpson was the architect of many fine courses throughout Europe during the early and middle part of the twentieth century.

Daniel Wexler authored *The Missing Links: America's Greatest Lost Courses and Holes* (2000).